PENTAGON PRAYER

PENTAGON PRAYER

Copyright © 2010 Dan Holdridge

www.danholdridge.com

www.pentagonprayer.com

Published by:

Blooming Twig Books LLC

PO Box 4668 #66675

New York, NY 10163-4668

www.bloomingtwigbooks.com

ISBN 978-1-933918-58-7

First Edition

10 9 8 7 6 5 4 3 2

PENTAGON PRAYER

DAN HOLDRIDGE

with **Rhesa Higgins**

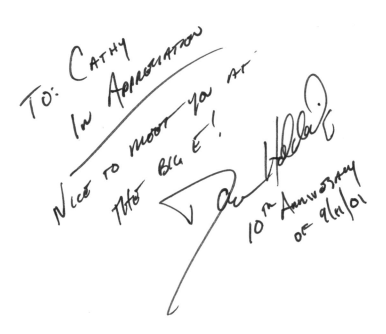

BLOOMING TWIG BOOKS
NEW YORK, NY

TABLE OF CONTENTS

DEDICATION

To THE 184 PEOPLE WHO DIED ACROSS THE wall from me on September 11th, 2001.

I should have been among you that day, were it not for the grace of God, and I live my life with a very clear understanding and appreciation for the fact that 184 mothers, fathers, sisters and brothers don't have the wonderful opportunity that I have today to live my life in love and gratitude for others.

Each and every person who died that day was a hero, and they teach us to be heroes in our daily lives. They have helped an entire nation rethink their own priorities in life.

Here is my definition of "hero": Help Everyone Regardless of the Outcome. Everyone in the Pentagon that day was working for a cause greater than him- or herself. A lot of times we think of heroes as firemen because they risk their lives each and every day. But then there are the everyday heroes who reach out to make someone else's life better, and the 184 people who died that day were heroes in every sense of the word.

PROLOGUE

ON THE CRYSTAL CLEAR MORNING OF SEP-
TEMBER 11, 2001 in Washington, D.C., I
followed my friend outside for a cigarette
break before we addressed the work orders on
our clipboards for the day. I had a dream job
at the Pentagon and was looking forward to
getting started on that day's work, not knowing that my life would soon change forever.

Standing in the cement zone just outside our
work area, I looked past the massive walls of
the Pentagon to the sun, and noticed that not
even a cloud was in the blue sky. For all I
knew, it was the beginning of another beautiful day.

I took a deep breath and pulled my cell phone
from my belt clip and leaned against the

outside wall as my friend Bobby Shelby lit his cigarette. I had heard about the attacks in New York that morning and I would have a chance to browse around on my cell phone and see the latest updates while Bobby smoked.

Seconds later, my cell phone was torn from my hands by a blast of air and an unfathomably powerful explosion. As I was thrown against the cement wall, windows were pulverized from five stories above me and the shards rained down on top of my exposed head. I used my clipboard as a shield from the falling glass.

The air was white with powdered cement. Far away my friend was screaming. Everything went black.

The airplane hit the side of the Pentagon at over 380 miles per hour; so much force that it nearly disintegrated. From what I've heard, the plane had been heading for the White House, but the terrorist pilots forgot two things. One, the Washington Monument was in the way. And two, the White House is surrounded by trees, so they couldn't come in at a clear angle;

the White House isn't visible from the sky, and huge buildings off Sixteenth Street and Seventeenth Street surround the White House on all sides. So when they decided not to go for the White House, they aimed for the next closest target, which was the Pentagon.

If the terrorists had hit the Pentagon from any other side, the death toll and carnage would have been worse than the New York attack. But they hit the most fortified side, the side that had been designed after the Oklahoma City bombing in 1995—the wall only a few hundred yards from where Bobby and I had stood while he smoked his cigarette.

If the building hadn't been fortified, I would be dead.

And only a few feet away from us, on the other side of the cement wall from where we had been standing, all 34 people died.

184 people died on that tragic day at the Pentagon. And I was not one of them.

A cigarette and a clipboard saved my life.

PART I

CHAPTER ONE

Clear Tuesday Morning

I COULD HEAR IT COMING.

There was a shhhzzz and then this huge "boom," accompanied by a tremendous burst of air. It was like standing right on the platform next to a speeding Amtrak train. This sonic blast came through and tossed me helplessly against the wall like a rag doll. And this invisible train was a long one. The blast just kept going and going and wouldn't stop.

All these forces were coming from different sides, and there was nothing I could do. There was a voice screaming over and over inside my head, "Stop it, stop it, stop it," praying that the blast would end. I wasn't really afraid; I had complete lack of control. There was nothing I could do except ride it out.

To my knowledge, I was the closest survivor to the epicenter of the blast. On the other side of that wall, everyone died. My friend, Bobby Shelby, and I were just plain lucky. If we had been a few feet in front or a few feet in back where there was an aluminum door, we would have died. That door was the size of a soda can after the blast. If we had been directly in front of the glass doors a few feet in the other direction, we would have died.

We had so many opportunities to die that day, and yet we didn't. Somehow we survived.

⊰✦⊱

I was living in Arlington, Virginia. I woke up in my one-bedroom apartment, which over-looked the city of Washington. I would wake up in the morning and open up the shades to the greatest city.

That day was no different than any others. I took the elevator down to the basement level where my rental car was parked and drove about a mile and half down the road to another garage underneath General Dynamics Corporation's headquarters for the Pentagon renovation program.

As I drove I wondered how many traffic lights I was going to hit this time. But, my commute is only about ten minutes. Some drive an hour and a half from upstate Maryland.

I dropped my stuff off at the office in Arlington and then went right outside again to catch the bus over to the Pentagon with my laptop in a carry-on luggage case and my backpack, as well as my security badge and my hardhat.

Once through security at the Pentagon, I was literally in a new world. The hallways there are stone, and wide enough that the Generals used to be able to drive a Jeep through them. But then they realized that the exhaust isn't good for you, so they stopped that practice. But that was how the Pentagon was originally designed.

The Pentagon first opened on September 11th, 1941. This particular day was the 60th anniversary of its opening, though there was no birthday cake at the entrance. It was just a workday for most of us, without any pomp or circumstance.

About an hour before the blast, I was hurrying to get to my telecommunication closet on the fifth floor. I had a conference call with Katie Jacques at 8:30 a.m. and the closet had a folding chair and insured good cell coverage and no interruptions. When I got there, florescent lights cast a harsh glare on the racks of electronic equipment behind me. They were waiting to be fired up for full-time use. I felt a sense of pride as I looked at that equipment. Months of our work had gone into having them ready for installation and operation in the Pentagon.

I slung my backpack on the floor and waited for the call. I had been working closely with Katie since I arrived at the Pentagon.

She was working in Durham, New Hampshire, for a company called Entersys Networks.

She was in charge of providing the Pentagon with new data networking equipment.

She and I used to have conference calls when I had my office up in Needham, Massachusetts. Those calls continued when I went down to the Pentagon. We worked together to learn what new equipment would be shipped our way, new advancements, anything I needed to know about, etc.

That morning, our conversation started like any other morning. I said to her, "Hey, how's it going? So what have we got on the plate?"

We talked about electronic equipment; for instance, this switch, that router, and the IP addressing scheme on this one, and then, after a brief time exchanging pleasantries, we hung up.

Our call that day had been faster than usual. I didn't need any new orders and the last order had arrived on time. I was so surprised when she called right back a few seconds after we had hung up.

"Hey, did you hear about New York?" she asked. "I just saw on the news that a plane crashed into the World Trade Center tower in Manhattan. Did you hear about it?"

Knowing that I was at the Pentagon, she was probably curious to see if I had heard anything about it here, at the center of American defense strategy. But it's a large building and I was on a renovation project, not a top-secret defense team. She was actually the first person to tell me about the attack that morning.

Only a few seconds into our conversation, she was watching as the second plane hit. She screamed into the receiver, "Oh my God, another plane just hit the other tower!"

Having grown up in Connecticut, I had been to New York many times. This was shocking enough that I wanted to get in touch with family members, or at least figure out what was going on.

"Katie, I've got to go." I said before hanging up.

My dad was having a normal workday at his electrical business office. He sounded surprised when he answered the phone.

"Hello? Dan?"

Though I was always close to my dad, I didn't call him regularly throughout the week. This was completely out of the ordinary. But I wanted to talk with him about New York. I wanted to talk with somebody in my family about the attack, and I thought about who might be home. As a schoolteacher, I knew my mother wouldn't be available at this time, so I called my dad, who I assumed would be at his office.

I hurriedly asked him, "Have you heard about New York? Are you watching the news?"

"No. What's going on?"

I told him, "Two planes flew into the World Trade Center towers. Get on the Internet and see what you can find out—I'm stuck here at work with no computer."

He started browsing and was soon absorbed in the news. He read me pieces of information as it was coming in. I wished I were at my desk in Virginia so I could see it for myself.

As we said goodbye, I reassured him that I was safe where I was.

"Don't worry about me, Dad. I'm in the Pentagon! This place is a fortress."

But I said it because I was nervous. I tried reassuring myself by saying to him, "I'm in the defense capital of the world... Of course I'm safe!"

That was the end of our conversation. At the end of the call, he said something like, "Well, let me know if anything goes on." Those might have been the last words I spoke with him had I died like the 184 people only a few feet away from me.

❧•❧

My dad had a barn, 48 acres, and was the leader of my local 4-H club. He taught me to be responsible at a very young age, and I remember how proud I was to pitch in around the farm.

When I was nine, I got my first little Jersey calf named Nan. I would feed her twice a day and make sure she had enough water. I would also walk her, which meant putting the halter on her and teaching her to get used to me. I would brush her as well. Soon she became my best friend. We communicated with each other in our own way. When she got old enough, I would milk her, and eventually, I grew my farm into eleven Jerseys, and Nan was the mother of almost all of them.

Every month, about thirty-five kids would show up in my family's huge living room for the 4-H meeting. We would organize all kinds of things there, from everyday kind of items to service projects.

"I pledge my head to clearer thinking, my heart to greater loyalty, my hands to larger service and my

health for better living, for my club, my community, my country and my world."

That's the 4-H pledge. Our 4-H motto: "To make the best better."

I joined 4-H when I was seven years old, and I've been involved ever since, from the bottom level all the way to the top. It's part of my life, an extended family, and it will always be that way. It's an amazing organization that gives children something to hang their hat on, learning leadership, citizenship and life skills.

In 1993 I was a tour guide for 4-H children in Washington, D.C. so I knew all 69 square miles pretty nicely.

That program was called Citizenship Washington Focus. I was a program assistant. Kids would come in on Sunday. That night we'd give them a night land tour of Washington, D.C. and then during the week we'd teach them about the three branches of the government and how it works. On Monday we would go for a tour to the Kennedy Center and Vietnam Memorial and Arlington Cemetery. Later in the week we would do three different sites like the Smithsonian, and a couple of others. We'd be working with these teens on how to make a differ-ence in their government and their country. We'd tell them that each person has a voice.

That was in 1993. I was 20 years old, going on 21. It was a summer internship job.

I went to a vocational technical high school and studied electronics. So, when I went to the Univer-sity of Connecticut, I actually thought I was going to be a sportscaster. After a semester of doing that and communicating with people that couldn't com-plete a sentence, I knew it wasn't for me. I worked for ABC Sports for a little bit, but that was short lived. It was eighteen weeks of effort, but that was when I learned what I didn't want to do in life.

My opportunity to do public relations at the NAS-DAQ stock market started in '95. After a year, I was interested in the computer engineering aspect. So I stayed late for a few months and just learned what they did. My boss saw the initiative I was taking, and then promoted me to an engineering spot. I worked at it for the next three years.

Soon after that, I got a call from my old college roommate to see if I wanted to work in Boston.

"Near the Red Sox?" I asked. "You bet."

I took a spot up there with General Dynamics as an assistant manager to the network engineering lab that designed the computer networks for the U.S. Marine Corps in 1999. In April 2001, I was asked to go down to the Pentagon and work.

Growing up on a farm, I used to wake up to do a day's worth of work before going to school. Then I'd go to school and I'd come home and do another day's worth of work, throwing bales of hay and feeding the cows.

Going to work at the Pentagon at 8 a.m. was a treat compared to the 5 a.m. wakeup time I had as a kid.

I loved my job. I couldn't believe they were paying me so well to do this kind of work.

I loved it in Washington, D.C.; there were so many things going on. It was an adventure. I would meet people, and they were all in there to change the world; it was just great.

There were concerts everywhere, and there was

always something going on. And then you see history in action: veterans coming up and crying at the Vietnam wall. It brings you back to reality in ways that you just don't get anywhere else.

I loved waking up there, anticipating my daily work. I had one of those jobs that made me feel like I was making a difference.

When a military general shakes your hand, telling you, "You did a great job," it's just incredible.

Soon I would be working as a contractor on Pen-Ren: contractor-speak for the multimillion-dollar 2001 renovation of the Pentagon.

It was the first major renovation that the building had since it opened in 1941. It was a complete upgrade to the entire facility, modernizing it and adding upgraded telecommunications and data networking.

The Pentagon was a 60-year-old system of five concentric buildings made of concrete. It housed over 23,000 office workers, and required security clearance to enter. Like pieces of a pie, the

Pentagon had been divided into five wedges for renovation. For the last six months, I had been working with a team of engineers to get the technology portion of the project finished on time. Our team was responsible for installing secure networks for the computers in Wedge 1, where the physical renovation was almost complete.

After my brief conversation with my father, I put my cell phone back on my belt and pulled out the two-way radio.

I spoke into the device: "Bobby, where are you?"

Bobby Shelby, a colleague and friend, met me at the escalators. We had worked side by side nearly every day that I had been at the Pentagon. As installation was nearing completion, we had become the computer guys that everyone needs. When computers wouldn't do their thing, we took the call.

The first thing I did was tell Bobby about the New York attacks. I said, "Hey Bobby, did you hear about New York?"

"No."

"A couple of planes hit the World Trade Center downtown just now."

"No kidding? Actual big planes, or small planes?"

"I guess big ones."

Both of us were shocked by the news and I suggested that we find out more in the Naval Command Center downstairs. I remembered that we had a network issue to take care of there anyway, so I told Bobby, "Alright, why don't we go there so we can see what's going on." The Command Center had big screens all across the room monitoring worldwide news broadcasts and situations.

There were two levels of security there. Once you entered a combination and swiped your ID card, you would find yourself in an intermediary area. After shutting the first door and swiping your card again at the second, you'd walk through, shut the door, and put in another combination on the other side. Then you were in a very secure area.

Inside, it was like a high-tech movie theater. If you looked to the right, there were huge movie theater-sized screens that showed pictures from all around the world. They were monitoring the world from in there. Behind the screens were rows of PCs, just as you would see in mis-sion control at NASA.

We had just finished setting up the computer networks in the office at the back of the Command Center. Any day prior to the 11th of September, we would have been inside that room, installing their networks.

Bobby asked if we could stop along the way for a quick cigarette break between the B and C rings, because it would prob-ably be a while until he had another chance to smoke.

Usually I wouldn't have joined Bobby, but I wanted to spend some time browsing on my phone's Internet browser to see what the latest news might be. We took the elevator down.

Bobby and I were so caught up in our conversation about New York that I forgot to put the clipboard of work orders back in my bag. I felt awkward carrying a clipboard with me but didn't want to go back to that communications closet to set it down. The elevator stopped on the fourth floor and a colleague joined us in the elevator. I immediately started telling him about New York. He was a technician who worked with us on the project.

"Did you hear about New York?" I asked.

As he responded "No" and began listening to the story, the door opened at the third floor, but he didn't get out.

I continued: "I got a phone call from Katie Jacques, and she told me about a couple planes that have hit the World Trade Center building."

"World Trade Center? In New York?"

"Yeah."

He was amazed. "No way."

When we arrived at the bottom floor, he got out and said, "This isn't my floor...I was supposed to get out on the third floor!"

We laughed with him and said, "Yeah, you missed your floor, dude! Didn't you see the door open on the third floor?"

He waved at us and started making his way back upstairs. "Oh, that's right. I'll just go up the escalator."

Only minutes later, he would be one of the guys who fell down the escalator when the explosion happened. His head was cut open on the escalator, but he survived. Who knows where he might have been if he had gotten off on the third floor. Maybe he wouldn't have survived.

After we said goodbye to our colleague, we headed towards the outdoor area where smokers commonly congregated, though it was empty that morning. We were only about ten feet away from the Naval Command Center when the plane would hit.

To my knowledge, no one in the Naval Command Center survived the attack. All 34 people died there while Bobby and I were outside on a smoke break. If Bobby hadn't asked me if he could stop and take a cigarette break, we would both be dead.

We went through the glass doors outside, into the sunshine of a beautiful Washington morning. I told Bobby I would read up on the attack on my cell phone while he smoked.

Looking straight up, I could see the clear blue sky above the five stories of concrete that surrounded me. The pavement beneath our feet was already heating up from the sun overhead. It wasn't unusual to look up and see airplanes coming in to land at Reagan International.

Bobby still had his backpack on. He lit up his cigarette with his arm up against the wall, looking at me while I described to him what was happening in New York; giving him the latest news from my cell phone's little browser.

We were in between the B and the C ring of Wedge 1, headed out toward the Naval

Command Center in the D ring. With the five concentric ring design of the Pentagon, we were right in the center of the building headed to the most outer ring. In the space between B and C there is an open area where vehicles can drive around on the inside. It was designed to keep exhaust out of office space and still get deliveries closer to the doors. But it had become a spot for smokers to take a break. The smoke didn't bother anyone out there and you could get cell service. The setting almost looked like prison yards in movies, with windows all looking down towards this area between the buildings.

I was wearing brown shoes, navy blue pants, and a collared tan shirt. The next time I would look down, my tan shirt would be colored with blood and my dark pants would look white from the powdered cement that stuck to the blood on them. My shoes would soon be grey with soot and debris.

Once we were outside, Bobby lit his cigarette. He was just a normal guy with red hair and a moustache. He was around the same age as I was, in his late twenties, and he smoked because of everyday stress.

That day he was wearing khaki pants and a collared shirt. But he looked a little bit disheveled, as if he had rolled out of bed that morning, having taken care of his kids on their way to school.

He and I were friendly; we would go out for beers every once in a while. I started up a Happy Hour thing when I was down there just because I was by myself. The guys who were married had to get what were called "kitchen passes" which would be when their wives gave them "permission" to go out after work.

So when Bobby got his kitchen pass we would go out, and chat about life. Bobby's the kind of guy people want to be friends with.

As far as a work colleague, he was smart and ambitious, and you couldn't ask for anyone better. I was really fortunate to work alongside him.

We talked about general things: things at work, things that were going on with his family, his wife's yearly visits to Japan with their two-year-old son to visit her side of the family. And I told him about my single life.

Bobby was doing his thing, smoking his morning cigarette, and I was doing my thing, reading my black Motorola flip phone, giving him a play-by-play of the attack on New York City.

"Holy crap," I said. "Bobby, there have got to be tons of people hurt there..."

At the time, I was kind of hoping that Bobby would hurry up on that cigarette so that we could get on with the day. We had several work orders that were piling up. Thank goodness Bobby took his time.

We stood outside the building with our steel-toed work boots. We had our company bright-orange hard hats on, with the words "General Dynamics" written across them in black bold lettering. I would never recover my hat from that day; it flew off my head or was knocked off, and I never saw it again.

I was focused on my cell phone, and there was the faint smell of freshly poured concrete in that area due to the construction. It was a scent I knew well; I worked in construction zones nearly every day.

At the moment, the news on cnn.com was still sketchy, but there was a picture of the second plane coming in and the thick smoke pluming from the other tower. There was time to think between each feed because the browser was moving so slowly, but I was impatient for more information. I updated Bobby with the news as it came in.

"They think it was a jet that flew into the buildings. Like, with people on it!"

"Thousands of people must be hurt!"

"What's next? The Pentagon?" I said before I returned to reading the news briefs, having no idea how prophetic my words would be.

Bobby started talking about the New York attack more heatedly. He was saying, "Geez, what kind of crazy person could get on a plane and run it into a building? That's ridiculous!"

Then 3, 2, 1, *boom.*

All hell broke loose.

The ground beneath my feet was gone. The walls and earth began to shake. I had no way to protect myself except for that cheap clipboard that I had forgotten to put away. I used it to protect my face from the glass and cement hailing down.

Bobby's cigarette rode a wave of glass and cement shards that hurtled past my face. I watched my cell phone shatter under the relentless pounding of the falling cement. The air turned white and then there was nothing.

It didn't even cross my mind that this monstrous explosion could have emanated from an airplane. I didn't know what it was at all. It happened so fast…

I just wanted it to stop. I prayed for it to stop. It wouldn't stop.

When debris started to hit me, it was coming from my left side; the direction of the blast. I used the clipboard in my hand as the hard hat blew off my head. The windows five floors above us were blown out where the plane was coming in. A shower of glass came down.

I don't think Bobby had anything to protect his head. I didn't see him during the actual blast, but he got a pretty large piece of glass stuck in his head. I had glass stuck in my arm where the clipboard wasn't there to protect me.

That clipboard saved my life.

There was cement mixed in with the glass; little chunks of cement and fine pieces of glass. Smaller pieces embedded into my skin, including the top of my head.

Once the glass hit, everything went white.

When I first woke up, I lay there and moved my left arm. I thought, *I can't feel it…* Then, I took a breath in. I said to myself, *I'm alive; I must be… I'm breathing…*

I just continued to breathe, despite the debris, dust and glass fragments in the air. It felt like breathing in fiberglass. I remember spitting a lot.

Being a computer techie, I often compare the moment when I first woke up after the blast to hitting the reset button on a computer. When you restart your computer, it first goes through your basic systems. I tried to figure out if anything was wrong with my hardware, so to speak.

How is my foot? I can move my foot. How is my arm? I can move it but I can't feel it... But I could breathe.

It looked like it was raining. Raining glass. I breathed in the deep, thick, powdery cement air, as if the very walls of the building had turned to dust that was now entering my lungs. The air reeked of what I later identified as jet fuel.

But all I thought about at the time was breathing. Bobby and I were both breathing this glass and cement in because that was all the air we had.

CHAPTER TWO

Escape from the Pentagon

I looked for Bobby. He was lying next to me and his face was covered in blood. He looked dazed. There were people screaming in every direction. I joined in long enough to say, "Holy shit! What the hell just happened?"

The ground was shaking so violently that I was afraid all of the concrete surrounding us was going to come down. The engineer in me began assessing the situation and looking for somewhere safe. The glass doors leading into C ring were missing but I saw a pillar that looked structurally sound and said, "Bobby!

Come on! We've got to get the hell out of here!" I grabbed Bobby's arm and pulled him toward the pillar.

We ran for the protection it offered. Bobby was bleeding from a cut on his head. I was shaking. Bobby still had his backpack on and it was grey with soot. The adrenaline made my heart pound and kept my mind sharp and clear. Safety was my only goal.

The air was full of pulverized concrete that clogged my nose and filled my lungs. The pungent smell of jet fuel and smoke made it difficult to breathe. The glass from every window in the building near me was flying everywhere and never seemed to land.

We got to the pillar and saw that a fireball was coming at us from the right. We made our way as best we could in the other direction, towards the center courtyard. Behind us was billowing smoke and fire. We could see fire through the windows of the doors twenty feet from where we had stood. We could see people were screaming and yelling, all running towards the center of the courtyard. I just kept thinking, over and over, *Gotta get out. Gotta get out.*

There was chaos all around. Over the top of all the screaming and yelling, I heard the fire alarms and loud horns going off. Deep down, I reached for the memory of the fire drills I had in school growing up.

People all over were shouting instructions. Pentagon security was running around, trying to get control of the situation.

Once we had gotten away from the fireball to relative safety, the pain started to settle in, and Bobby and I collapsed on one of the benches.

One of my colleagues came over and said, "Holy crap, you've been hit!" People just started screaming, "You've been hit, you've been hit." I didn't know what that meant. But both Bobby and I were pretty messed up. Bobby had a good cut on the top of his head, and he was bleeding like a stuck pig. It looked terrifying to people.

Although I didn't have as gruesome a wound as Bobby, my shirt was covered with blood. But I still wasn't registering what it all meant.

My colleagues shouted at us, "What do you need? What do you need?"

Overwhelmed and feeling pain all over my body, I could only respond, "Uh...I don't know." It had only been a few minutes since we had been thrown from the blast and showered with glass, and we were horrified that the fireball would soon engulf the entire building. It was chaos, and we had escaped the worst of it with our lives, but we still needed to get out of there, despite our pain. Rescue teams were commanding people where to go, but all I heard was the endless deafening drone of the fire alarm.

Bobby and I sat there in pain, paralyzed by the thought, *What just happened?* We were blinded by our shock, and I felt throbbing pain all through my whole left side. It was excruciating.

"We've got to get out of here! We've got to get out of here..." Everyone around us was shouting for us to move, propping us up and telling us to get out. No one knew if a second attack was coming, or if more explosions would rock the courtyard, or if the fire would overtake the building. The evacuation, if you could call it that, was completely unorganized, though there was no lack of people shouting directions.

B.J. Meadows, a friend from our renovation team, saw us there. He had been on the fifth floor and was unhurt. He put my arm around his shoulders and became my human crutch for the long walk out to the lawn of the Pentagon. Someone grabbed Bobby, too, and we got separated in the chaos.

I struggled to walk down a lane that we thought was the exit, only to find that it was a dead end. We had to turn around, and we went down another corridor. I felt like we would never escape this nightmare. There are 18 miles of corridor in the Pentagon, and it would be easy to get lost in the confusion. But there was no alternative. I had to press on. On a normal day, where the blast occurred would have been a 15- or 20-minute walk to get out of the building. But on this day, everyone was going in different directions, screaming in terror, not knowing if they would live or die; blood and noise was all around.

As I was being helped out of the building by Meadows, I tried to grab everyone's cell phones. I had this uncontrollable impulse to call home and tell everyone that I was alive. At that point, I was also trying to convince myself the same thing. I held onto the thought that talking to a loved one would have confirmed that everything was going to be all right. So I reached out and tried to pull cell phones off the belts and out of the hands of anyone we passed by. I ended up getting several phones, though all of the phones' owners shouted to me that they wouldn't work anyway.

I could barely focus on staying conscious, let alone remembering phone numbers.

I later wondered if the phone, which had been open to the news of the New York City attack, had ironically showed the news of the Pentagon blast as it lay buried in the rubble where it was knocked out of my hands.

I mostly kept my eyes shut against the pain as Meadows dragged me out of the building with little help from me. It was as if somebody had hit me with a car on the left side... It was so intense. With every step I was praying, *Just let the pain stop...*

It was a throbbing pain, and I couldn't really tell where it was coming from. It was as if my entire body felt like a finger slammed in a car door. I knew I had been hit by cement, glass and everything else, but I couldn't look into a mirror to see where I was hurt. My body was numbed by the pain and adrenaline coursing through my bloodstream.

My grandfather on my father's side was my hero, mentor and friend. I still think about him nearly every day, even though he died in the autumn of 1988 at age 64. I was crushed at the time, as a

teenager. He died of a massive heart attack at home while chopping wood.

During the summer of 1986, I worked with him to build my father's barn. It still stands today, and reminds me of that summer every time I visit my parents. He was an incredibly strong guy in his words and spirit, and, of course, his arms, shoulders and back. I wanted to grow up to be just like him. When I went over to his house, nothing else in the world mattered. He was just an amazing man.

One of my favorite memories is when he would have a pack of gum in his shirt pocket that I would have to dive for. If he didn't have one, I'd look at him, and he would say, "You know where they're stored." So, I would get a chair and reach for the right-hand-side cubbyhole above the stove where he kept his gum. He made sure that my grandma had that well stocked at all times.

What my grandfather taught me went far beyond his altruistic view about sharing gum with his grand-children. He taught me how to appreciate life in his own unique way. He would show me the kind of man I could be, not just tell me. While I was helping him build my father's barn that summer, my grandfather would be hanging off the front side of the barn by a 2x4 that he had tacked onto the roof. While he was hammering the other side of it, I said, fearful of my grandfather's safety, "Grandpa, aren't you worried about falling?"

He told me, "If I do my job right, I don't have anything to worry about." That will stick with me for the rest of my life.

That was confidence! I was amazed by my grandfather's strong statement, and I have lived by it ever since, though I've never quite had as much courage as he did. In a similar situation, I would harness myself in, but there was my 62-year old grandfather, simply hanging off of a board two stories above the earth, working steadily to the amazement of his gape-mouthed grandson below.

It's one thing to appreciate life, and it's a whole other thing to show and do things. He built things all around town, including an addition onto his church's building. Although my grandfather died at a young age, he was still able to show his appreciation for his neighbors, friends and even

complete strangers every day, through his actions,
not just his talk.

When B.J. led me out of the doors of the Pentagon after what seemed like an eternity, the daylight was so bright I had to close my eyes. Sirens were sounding all around us. The air was warm and thick with humidity. B.J. saw a large group of government official coats and people lying on the grass. He continued to support me as we headed in that direction.

A makeshift triage area had been set up on the lawn. B.J. helped me lay down on the grass, then he went to find medical personnel.

The air was full of thick black smoke that burned my nose, mouth and eyes. It was also filled with the smells of jet fuel, pulverized cement, and burning flesh. The smoke wasn't dark enough to hide the injured people all around me. There was a hole in the building and huge flames still devoured the walls that were standing.

When I first looked up from the grass where B.J. set me down, I could see the clear blue sky, with F-16 fighter jets turning figure-eights. They were like a hornet's nest, flying around and around us in protective formation.

I don't recall ever seeing fighter jets like that, besides maybe at an air show. You could tell they were engaged. They were circling and protecting the skies above our heads. There was nothing in the air that would fly unnoticed.

All around me, people were getting sewn back together. It was grotesque. Surgeon generals of the armed services, medics from the Arlington Fire Department, and anyone else who knew first aid were helping out where they could. There were a lot of people running around asking where they could donate blood. We were lucky that these people were trained for triage. Because the Pentagon is a military institution, all of these medics and doctors had experience in the field. This was a battlefield, and they knew what to do. Even though I have never been a soldier, I was in the middle of a war zone on American soil.

I've talked to a lot of veterans who ask me about the aftermath of the attack.

"So, does it stick with you at nighttime? Do you have a tough time sleeping?"

I tell them, "Yes, I have a hard time sleeping."

"Oh yeah," they tell me. "That will never leave you..."

I was hoping that someone would tell me, "Time heals everything." That's what we hear all the time, and that's what I wanted to hear more than anything.

Now I know that what veterans say is true. I still have nightmares, and I still have a hard time sleeping many nights. It makes me think of all of the veterans around the country and around the world who have the same curse that I have; they can never forget the trauma of those horrific scenes in battle. And these men and women would do this on a daily basis. Soldiers have their own 9/11 on a regular basis. I can't fathom how they handle it.

There were people on the lawn near me who had their body cavities opened up under the clear skies that day. I turned my head to the left and to the right from where I lay, and I could see the carnage all around me. They were in tremendous pain, and doctors were doing what is called "instant surgery." The ambulances couldn't come fast enough. It was horrible, but I will never forget it. People were fighting for their very lives in every direction; their blood spilling out onto the green grass of the Pentagon's lawn. I couldn't stand to see the blood anymore. So I looked up.

I was trying to understand why I couldn't feel my left hand and arm. And my leg. I attempted not to focus on my own pain or the screams all around me, but I couldn't help but worry about my wounds.

After a while, I had to realize that I couldn't be in control of everything. In fact, I had no control over the situation, and I had to reach for help somewhere else. That's when I started to pray.

In my opinion, atheists and people who don't have a true appreciation for religion crave and hope and ask for help from a higher power when the situation calls for it and there's no other place to turn. They might say, "Just give me one more day, one more moment." And that is a prayer for help.

They gave us all little ribbons around our wrists, so the medics would know whom to help first. The red ribbons were first, the yellows were second, and the greens were third. They gave me a green ribbon. I knew I would be all right. I stared up into the sky and prayed softly to myself, hoping to shut out the screams all around me.

I need help, God. If there's ever a moment that I need help, it's right now. I prayed for the people next to me whose screams I was attempting to mask with the silent words in my mind: *These people all around me need your help. We all need hope. Whatever it is that I need to do, we just need You now.* I repeated those words over and over, focusing on hope and light, hoping that the suffering would soon be over for all of us on the green grass.

There were people who were dead or dying right next to me. There was confusion and chaos all around. People were shouting, "The White House was hit, the State Department was hit!"

As I continued to pray, my thoughts drifted away from the horror of the present, to thoughts of home and growing up on our farm. Images of cows, pastures, barns and family filled my head and distracted me from the blood and smoke surrounding me. I thought about my niece, who was due to be born any day now, and how I was going to be her godfather.

I was in a war zone on American soil. On my left were men and women with over half of their bodies burned. People's stomachs were opened and being operated on, right there. Clothing was melted to bodies, and some victims had no skin left.

Doctors and paramedics hovered over patients. While I waited for someone to come back and tell me what to do, the throbbing in my left side started to go numb. I lost all sense of time and reality.

The sounds of the blast, then screams, repeated endlessly in my head. Walkie-talkies sounded orders being given to firefighters, who wore them on their belts. Emergency medical personnel swarmed the courtyard in uniforms, shouting instructions to victims and one another.

Panicked, faceless people shouted at each other in the crowd.

Reality set in again when a paramedic came up running and shouted, "There's a second plane incoming, get the hell out of here."

Bobby and I stumbled alongside an EMT about 25 yards from the lawn of the Pentagon to take shelter under the bridge to Route 395 near the triage unit. This dedicated paramedic continued to bandage Bobby's head. When she finished, she headed back to triage.

We attempted to fight through the pain as we braced ourselves for another explosion.

At a loss for anything else to do, I prayed to God for protection from a second plane.

The deep rumble of an engine made me jump. Was this the first hint of the next plane on its way?

Then we saw the sound was emanating from a grey SUV driving beneath the underpass, headed directly toward us. The small blonde driver looked tiny in her giant car. She stopped, rolled down the passenger window and said gently but firmly, "Get in. I'll take you to the hospital."

The prayers I had been repeating in my head like a mantra hadn't stopped even as we took our position at the underpass. As an answer to those prayers, our guardian angel, Erin Anderson, came driving up in her SUV.

She told us, "I don't know what exactly made me drive here, but I'm here to take you to the hospital."

I responded to her quickly. I said, "Get out of here, there's a second plane incoming."

But despite my urging, she helped us into her car. I climbed into the back seat and Bobby got in the passenger side of the front seat. She turned around to look me square in the eye and reassured us again that she would get us to the hospital.

Despite her reassurances, she was just as nervous as we were. Imagine what she must have seen in Bobby and me; we were so messed up, bleeding into our bandages, covered in soot and ash and shards of glass.

Our tiny blonde angel floored that huge SUV and got us out of there. She sped away from the Pentagon with purpose.

We were too afraid to even look back as smoke filled the back window and shouts faded into the distance. All I could think was that we needed to get moving before another plane came in.

Still weak from shock, I kept looking at my left hand, trying to piece together what had just happened. I was riding in her car and kept looking at and twisting my left hand, thinking, *I can't feel it, I can't feel it.*

The cut on Bobby's head was pretty bad. I remember seeing his bloody hair from the back seat.

I think she must have been talking with Bobby up front. I remember she said something like, "Does your family know you're okay?"

I just kept my head back, trying to stave off the throbbing pain all over my body. As shock wore off, the pain took over. It was excruciating.

Most of the victims went to the Walter Reed Medical Clinic in Washington, but we were heading to the Fort Myers Medical Clinic.

My journey was just beginning as we sped away from the ruins of my former life. In the next hours and days, I attempted to rejoin the world, though nothing seemed to function as it should. Things had changed.

CHAPTER THREE

Guardian Angel

WHEN I FIRST STARTED SPEAKING ABOUT MY *experiences, I was scheduled to present at a public event at the National 4-H Center in Washington. I invited Erin Anderson to come to the event, but she indicated to me she couldn't attend due to her schedule. I certainly didn't expect her to be there in the audience.*

I explained to the crowd, "There's a little bit of Erin Anderson within each of you. You all have the ability to make a difference by doing something that at the time seems small. By simply driving Bobby and me to the hospital in her SUV, she impacted thousands of people. Everyone in this audience is now touched by what she did, because she changed my life. And you can all impact thousands of people by the little things you do to help and appreciate one another every day."

Delivering hope to others will answer people's prayers.

I continued: "If I could only just tell Erin Anderson how what she did will impact thousands of people… She was truly my guardian angel that day, and I wish she could hear what that meant to me."

At that moment, someone in the audience stood up.

"Dan, I made it… I'm here."

It was Erin Anderson. Everyone there that afternoon was moved to tears, including me. That moment changed the rest of my life.

Each of us can be an agent for hope in this world as Erin was for Bobby and me.

In Rhode Island, my sister, Amy, called my dad at work.

"Dad? Have you been watching the news? Is Dan okay?" she asked.

"I just talked to Dan. He's fine," Dad answered.

"You talked to Dan since the Pentagon was hit and he's okay?" she asked.

"The Pentagon was hit? What? Are you sure? The Pentagon? I've got to go, Amy."

Dad hung up on Amy and immediately dialed my cell phone. My voice mail picked up. He hung up and looked for my work number, the number for my company's main office in Massachusetts.

"Good morning, General Dynamics," a cheerful receptionist answered.

"My son works for your company and is stationed at the Pentagon. I need to know if he is okay."

"Well, sir, I'm not sure about that but I'm going to transfer you to security and see if they can help you. Please hold."

Elevator music played. Dad nervously tapped his fingers on his desk.

"This is the security department. How can I help you?" a kind voice answered.

"My son works for General Dynamics and is stationed at the Pentagon. He didn't answer his cell phone and I need to know if he is okay! Please help me find him."

"Sir, no one in the Pentagon has gotten word to us yet. Phone companies are telling us that circuits are completely overloaded. He probably just hasn't been able to call yet."

"I need to know. Who else can I talk to?" My father is a man defined by action, not waiting, just like his father.

"What is your son's name, sir? Maybe I can transfer you to his boss."

"Daniel Holdridge."

"Okay. Please hold."

More elevator music. More drumming fingers.

Dad's foot began to twitch in frustration.

"Hello, this is Barbara. I am an assistant to the V.P. of the company. How can I help you, sir?"

"Barbara, my son works for your company. He is stationed at the Pentagon and I need to know if he is okay."

"Yes, your son's name is Daniel Holdridge. Is that correct?"

"Yes, ma'am."

"What is your name, sir?"

"My name is James Holdridge."

"Okay, Mr. Holdridge. We have not been able to reach anyone at the Pentagon, including Dan's supervisor. What I am going to do is try to reach other offices in the country and see if anyone has had word from them. I need you to hold and trust that I am doing my best to reach them. Is that okay?"

"Thank you. Yes, I'll hold."

⇒✦⇐

Would we feel impact from another plane? Would the highway shake? Would the force push even this giant SUV forward?

Panic began to rise in my chest as these thoughts throbbed across my mind. "Relax and breathe," I muttered to myself in the backseat.

Our SUV-driving hero was still barreling down the highway and looking intently at the road ahead of us.

Where was she taking us?

Within minutes we pulled up to the Fort Myer's clinic. The gates were closed and armed guards stood beside them. One of the uniformed men approached the driver's window holding his huge rifle in front of him. The angel lady rolled down the window and took off her sunglasses to look him straight in the eye.

"This facility is locked down, ma'm. No one

gets in or out." His tone was matter-of-fact and his voice even.

"I have my ID with me; my husband works as a naval officer. These men were injured at the Pentagon and need medical attention. Please let us through." She was calm and efficient in her explanation.

"I'm sorry but I have orders to keep this place secure. You will have to leave." He sounded genuinely sorry.

"Sir, look at this man." She pointed to Bobby's head. "He needs to see a doctor. At least look at my ID before you send us away."

"One moment, please." He took her ID to the gatehouse. The windows were darkened and we couldn't see what he was doing while inside but just a moment later he came back out. "Okay, the hospital is just inside the gates, on your left. Go straight there." He handed back the ID as the gates opened. They put mirrors under the car and inspected the SUV prior to allowing us to enter.

She smiled calmly and pulled through.

My heart was pounding. I felt my breaths get shorter and faster again. Why was this facility on lockdown? What was going on?

Breathe in, breathe out. I told myself. *Calm down. We're in now. Help is near.*

My legs were seizing up again as the adrenaline ebbed away. I mentally prepared myself to walk inside the hospital, willing my legs to move when I ordered them.

After the car was parked, I struggled out of the backseat to help Bobby. He seemed dazed. We were required to use wheelchairs to go through the sliding glass doors into a blast of air conditioning. The kind, white-haired volunteer behind the admissions desk immediately moved into action when she saw us. A nurse came to us and Bobby was whisked back to a room.

I was given paperwork to fill out which I chose to work on outside the entrance of the hospital. The cold air and fluorescent lights of the waiting room left my muscles more tense and my head pounding. Our rescue driver came outside with me.

"I'm Erin, by the way. Erin Anderson." She smiled and stuck out her hand.

"I'm Dan Holdridge. It's nice to meet you." We shook on it and settled into the business of hospital forms; she even did some of the writing when I couldn't control the pen.

After the forms were complete and I was waiting to be seen by the medical staff, I became acutely aware, again, of the fact that my family didn't know where I was. Bobby's wife and kids didn't know where he was or if he was even alive. I started hyperventilating again as the feelings of isolation rushed over me. My cell phone was at the bottom of a pile of rubble in a burning building. I didn't have anyone's phone numbers. Surely the Pentagon was on the news by now. My family would be frantic. My breathing became completely erratic.

"Dan? Are you hurting? Do you want me to go get a nurse?" Erin looked at me intensely.

"I need to call my family," I huffed out while trying to control my breathing. "I haven't reached them yet. My cell phone is gone. Bobby has a wife and kids. They don't know where we are. I need to call. I don't have a phone. I don't have their numbers. I'm helpless."

"Okay, let me see what I can do."

In Connecticut, my mother, an elementary school teacher, found her principal knocking at her classroom door.

"Mrs. Holdridge, can you please come out in the hallway."

The students started to buzz immediately with giggles and speculations about why their teacher was in trouble.

"Class, I expect you to wait quietly. I'll be back." The whispers died down after her firm words.

Once out in the hallway, the door firmly closed behind them, the principal gently placed his hand on my mom's shoulder. "Cathy, we have some news that I need to tell you. We have just learned that the United States Pentagon was hit by an airplane. We know your son works there, and no one has heard if he made it out alive."

Mom began to shake, and then cry.

"My son? My baby? God, please let nothing bad happen to my son. Please God!"

The sobs continued to consume her body and the principal arranged for a substitute to take over her class. He found her a quiet place to wait and soon she was joined by her sister, Jane. Together they waited and wondered and prayed.

The two-way radio on my belt crackled to life. I had forgotten it was there.

"Dan? Dan Holdridge? This is Tom. Dan, are you there? Over."

I picked it up and said, "This is Dan. Tom, Bobby and I are alive. Over."

"Man! I'm glad to hear from you! Where are you? Over."

"Bobby and I are at the Fort Myer's clinic. Over."

"Are you okay? How's Bobby? Over."

"We are both getting checked out. Over."

"Let us know when you know something. Over."

"Will do. Over and out."

Erin had gone back into the waiting room. Her face was pale and her eyes red. I sat down next to her and waited.

"My husband is in the Navy and he was just deployed for at least a year," she said, turning towards me. He's already on board and I can't see him. Would you mind if I stayed with you today?"

"Erin, my family is all the way in Connecticut. Would you stay with me today?"

For nearly an hour, we watched as other victims from the day made their way into that clinic. Finally, a nurse came out and told us that Bobby was going to be transferred to another hospital that could take care of the cut on his head. But, he wanted to see us before he left. I followed the nurse back to Bobby's bed.

As soon as he saw me he said, "Dan, this is my home phone number and my parent's phone number. Please call them. Please tell them that I'm alive. They can meet me at the hospital." He handed me a slip of paper.

"I'll do it. I'll find a phone to use. Go! Get help for that cut and I'll call. Take care. I'll see you soon."

The nurse wheeled him out of the room and Erin found a doctor who let us use his office phone. Bobby's wife answered on the first ring. She was crying.

"This is Dan Holdridge. I work with Bobby. Bobby is on his way to the hospital for a cut on his head and he wants you to meet him there. He's going to be okay."

"He's okay. He's okay. He's okay!" The sobs started again as I told her the name of the hospital and asked if she could find it.

In Connecticut, my dad was getting desperate for answers. It had been more than an hour since the blast and he still had no word.

"Mr. Holdridge? This is Barbara again. I've got a group working to reach your son. Here's what's going on: I called a former colleague of his in Arizona who had a more direct number into the Arlington, VA office. The Arlington office has two-way radios. They are trying to contact Dan through the radio. We hope to hear soon. Please keep holding."

I borrowed a doctor's phone at the hospital, and that was how I was first able to call my family and tell them I was safe. My parent's house was the only number that I could remember. I didn't think anyone would be home on a weekday morning but I could at least leave them a message and tell them where I was.

I was quickly fading because of the pain medication. Erin worried that I would forget what I had just dialed, so she wrote down my parents' telephone number on my hospital bed's sheets.

My brother happened to be at my parents' house. I was lucky to get through on this borrowed telephone. But I didn't know what to say. How could I tell my brother that I had lived through a terrorist attack? How could I tell him that I needed help and comfort?

After my brother answered, I responded with only his name.

"Jim."

Recognizing my voice, he immediately asked, "Are you okay?"

I told him, honestly, "I don't know."

Then I felt compelled to ask him what had happened to me. As strange as it may sound, no one had explained to me what had happened. Perhaps they were all shielding me from the truth, or more likely, they probably thought that I knew what had happened. Yet, all I knew at that point was that I had almost died when an airplane hit the Pentagon.

So I asked Jim, "What happened?"

He responded in surprise, "What do you mean, 'What happened?'" He was amazed that I didn't know the magnitude of what I had just been through.

"Man," I said, "we heard so many things that I have no idea what really happened. We heard all kinds of things: it was a small plane, a helicopter, a big plane... What actually happened?"

"A huge plane hit the Pentagon."

"You mean one of those 757 jets?" I asked in amazement.

I finally understood why the blast had been so huge, and why I had smelled jet fumes, why the whole building behind us had been decimated. I said under my breath, "Holy crap," the biggest expletive I could muster at the time.

"Where are you?" he asked.

"In the hospital."

At that point, my brother, thinking that I had survived the attack, and not realizing I had actually been hurt, hurriedly said, "What the hell for?"

Now he was worried. His little brother had been hit.

"What is the matter?"

"Jim, I was hit."

He was listening in stunned silence.

"Jim, I don't know what's wrong," I continued.

"I'm in a lot of pain, but I'm going to be okay. I'm in the hospital now. They're giving me shots for the pain and doing evaluations on me right now."

Eager to get off the subject of my well-being, I gave Jim a mission.

"Grab Mom's Rolodex and call everyone in there and tell them I'm alive, and spread the word that I'm alive."

You can imagine how shocked my brother was at that moment, and how quickly he ran to the Rolodex and called every name in the book, building a team of support and prayers that surround me still to this day.

My brother and I were never the touchy-feely type. Usually, we talked about the Red Sox and that was about it. But he is my older brother, and it's impossible to even explain how close our bond is. We would do anything for each other.

I asked him if anyone was at home.

"Mom's at school, waiting to hear and Aunt Jane is with her," he replied. "Amy's been calling every little while but she didn't want Brendan to get too frightened so she's at home. Dad has been on the phone with General Dynamics trying to find you."

"Call them all, okay? I'll try to call back when I see a doctor. Make sure someone is by the phone because this is the only number I could remember."

I hung up and sobbed with relief. The loneliness washed over me as I realized how far away they were. I wanted to see them so much it literally hurt.

I lay back on the hospital bed, moving slowly. My left side was throbbing again from my shoulder to my toes.

The doctors began to assess my injuries. I kept telling them that my left side throbbed with pain and then would go numb. It happened over and over.

Finally, a grandmotherly nurse with a soft face and empathetic eyes told me that she was going to give me a shot for the pain.

"Will it make me groggy?" I asked.

"Yes, it might. But you won't be hurting anymore," she told me.

When I was 21 in the summer of 1994, I was the program director of a local 4H Camp in Connecticut. One day I was called urgently to the nurse's office; she explained to me that one of the campers who had been in the fishing program area had a fishhook caught in his thumb. That's about the most painful anything can be; the thumb is, after all, one of the most sensitive places in the human body. I said to the nurse, "Why don't we just pull it out?" But when I actually saw the hook in the boy's finger, I knew that we would have to bring him to the hospital. It was embedded deep within the flesh of his thumb, and there would be no way to remove the jagged object without causing a great deal more suffering.

Each summer, the campers would build their own fishing poles with a kit that we provided them. This longtime camper had tried to take the barbed hook out of a fish's mouth, following safety guidelines, but something slipped, and the hook dug deep into the flesh of his thumb.

I had never seen anything like this before. I could see the terrible pain he was in, and I wanted to help him, but there was nothing I could do but sit with him. We drove him to the local hospital and brought him into the emergency room waiting area, where we soon saw the triage nurse. Of course I notified his parents, and they soon came down as well.

I had learned early on as a counselor, and now as a program director, that humor helped more than anything else to calm people down. I use humor in 99.9% of all stressful situations, whether it be mine or others. It's just who I am.

The first thing I said to my 11-year old friend was, "It looks like you caught a big one!" The poor little guy probably didn't need humor at that point, but that was my first response.

"Yeah, it really hurts," he told me.

"Well, it probably hurt the fish more!" I said to the small, accident-prone camper. I reassured him that everything would be okay and sat with him so that he wouldn't be scared. My job was to make him smile on the inside, because on the outside he was hurting.

"Now, time for this shot."

"Where are you going to put that shot?" I asked.

She smiled and replied, "Right where you think I am."

I quipped up, "You just want to look at my butt!"

"I've seen quite a few of those in my time!" she laughed.

The nurse, Erin Anderson, and I laughed like it was the funniest thing ever said.

Later, a chaplain began making rounds. I heard him praying with others around me who had also been in the Pentagon.

From my bed, I could hear a woman nearby who had been on the floor above impact and had seen the plane coming in and hitting the building right under her feet.

Her army uniform was still crisp and professional but her face was frantic with grief. The chaplain was gentle and reassuring as he talked with her.

I felt a deep sense of peace in the midst of all this chaos to hear his words of comfort.

He approached me with understanding on his face. "What's your name, son?"

"Daniel," I replied, even though I had gone by Dan or Danny my entire life.

It was as if using my full name would endear me more to God and to this kind man's prayers. He smiled the most calm, benevolent smile I've ever seen. There was so much comfort in his smile.

"You know that story about Daniel in the lion's den, right?" he asked.

"Yes, I heard that one growing up. I know it well." I told him.

As soon as the chaplain began speaking about the Daniel story, I was able to revert to the warm memories of my childhood when I had first learned that story.

He continued, "That all worked out pretty well for Daniel, don't you think?"

"Yes, I do. But do you think Daniel felt guilty for being saved when others had died in that same place?"

"I don't know. The Bible doesn't tell us that. Do you feel guilty, Daniel?"

Then he asked me, as if inviting me into a gentle circle of prayer, "Do you mind if I hold your hand?"

"No, no. Go ahead," I said. As he held my hand from the chair next to me, we just talked.

"A lot of people died today. People who had families, kids. People who were younger than me, smarter than me, better than me. Why did they die? Why did I live?" The questions had been circling in my mind since I hung up the phone with Jim.

"Those are hard questions, Daniel. I don't think anyone can answer them for you."

What the chaplain told me next I will never forget: "I believe that if you will keep praying, God will answer you."

Hungry for hope, I felt the comfort of his words: "Keep praying. Keep asking. God won't get tired of your asking."

With his incredible calm, the chaplain touched my arm and said, "I'll be praying for you, Daniel."

PART II

CHAPTER FOUR

Home

WHEN THE PAIN MEDICINE KICKED IN, AND as my shock wore off, I was able to have a longer conversation with my mysterious rescuer, Erin Anderson. She sat down near me and started asking me about my family.

It was then that I realized that she had done something far beyond the realm of the ordinary. She had rescued Bobby and me from the burning inferno. I had to ask her what had compelled her to leave the comfort of her home and enter a battle zone.

"Why did you come?" I asked. "Does your husband work at the Pentagon? Were you looking for him?"

Erin shook her head and answered simply, "I was home, watching TV. I saw all the horrible pictures from New York and then suddenly they were talking about the Pentagon."

This was in her backyard, and she felt that she had to do something: "So I got in my car and drove down there."

"How did you find us?" I asked.

"When I got to the Pentagon, there were tanks and armored men blocking the road. They told me that everything was locked down, no one in or out.

I showed the soldiers my military ID and said that I was going in. They did their best to stop me, but I kept telling them that I could help the injured. Finally they let me through. A minute later I saw you guys crouched underneath that underpass."

"Thank you. Thank you for coming to get us," I said. My words seemed so inadequate.

Not long after, the doctors released me with prescriptions for the pain but no real answers as to why I was hurting. Nothing was broken and there were just surface scratches and bruising. I didn't question them for long. I was too tired.

Erin drove me to the General Dynamics headquarters there in Virginia. I grabbed a few of my things and saw my colleagues. They had been worried about Bobby and me all day. I realized that I didn't want to be alone at home that night. One of my friends offered me a place with his family for as long as I needed it.

Charlie Grow's family made me feel right at home. It was soothing to have a warm meal and a place to sleep among people who loved each other.

It dawned on me to call my cell phone to check the messages. Even though the phone was destroyed, my number was still active. I had almost 50 messages that night.

"Dan, are you okay? I saw about the Pentagon. Call me!"

"Dan, were you at work today? Are you alright? Please call me."

"Dan, I'm worried about you after seeing all the coverage. Call me!"

None of them left their phone numbers! I didn't have any way to get back in touch with them. So, I changed the outgoing message:

"You have reached Dan. I am alive after the attacks on the Pentagon. My phone was ruined and I don't have your number. Please call my parent's home for updates and leave your number with them. I'll try to return as many calls as I can. Thank you."

An hour later, I checked the messages again. There were several and all they said was, "Thank God you are alright!"

I first spoke with my parents later that night from my colleague's home. Crying the whole time, I spoke to them each in turn, and I let them know that I was alive. They had only seen what was on television, so they knew it was really bad, and they were in shock that I had been in the middle of the blast.

My mom, attempting to organize the good will and prayers of friends and family, and wanting to somehow give me a motherly bear hug from afar, listed off the people who had all called their home, telling me how they all had me in their thoughts.

"Do you remember this person?" she asked. "They tracked you down and they called here. And this person and this person, do you remember them? They called, too."

Parents aren't supposed to outlive their kids. I am their youngest son, and she couldn't bear to think that I was gone, that she wouldn't be able to hug me one more time, or cradle the children I might have someday in her arms.

She's been an educator since I was very young. She started out as a teacher's aide, and she went to school while raising us and got her teacher certification.

Since then, she's been loved for decades by her classrooms of children. Parents call to ask for her as their child's teacher. They know that when Cathy Holdridge is going to be the teacher of their child, their child will have a second mother who will care for them in ways that they can't fathom. My mom is somebody that has more compassion and care than anyone I know on this earth. Her big heart was easily broken that day when she thought I might not have made it through the attack.

She had sat and prayed until she heard the news from my father that I was alive, and heard from my brother that I had spoken to him. She and my dad wanted me home so that they could take care of me and make sure that I would be all right.

My dad was pretty shaken up over the phone.

"Well, I'm glad you're okay. We're going to try and get you home." He stayed strong for me, and he found a way of getting me home.

My dad has a fierce ability to take care of his loved ones. When my grandfather died, and my brother was in the military, my dad talked to the Red Cross to get him home for the wake. When that didn't work, he called my brother's drill sergeant directly. I don't think the drill sergeant understood he was dealing with a swamp-Yankee farmer.

"If we're not at war, my son's going to come home, and he's going to pay respects to his grandfather, and then you can have him back. I don't give a damn about what protocols and priorities you have, sir, he's coming home. And if I have to come down there and get him, I will come down there and get him."

He was eventually successful, and my brother was there to mourn for my grandfather.

I'm sure my brother had to pay for that later on, but he was going to come home for my grandfather's funeral, come hell or high water.

It had taken my family 90 minutes to find out that I was alive. Imagine the gut-wrenching feeling that was going on inside of them. 90 minutes, not knowing whether I was dead or alive.

A lot of people who heard that I hadn't been accounted for prayed for me. But my dad is not really a religious man. He's more of a man of action. He was the guy who was calling security and talking his way up the line until he finally could get through to someone who got through to someone else who finally found out that I was alive.

Everyone who saw my dad that day said that he was on a mission. He was going to find me, one way or another. He's an engineer, and engineers find solutions.

❖

Although I had been taken in for the night, the love and support of my own family seemed very far away. That first telephone conversation helped, if only a little, to calm

me down. It was an incredible experience to
realize that so many people cared about me
that much.

After I hung up the phone with my parents
that night, there was nothing on the television except more replays of the attacks and
recovery efforts. I couldn't take any more, so
I headed up to take a shower. I just wanted to
do something normal.

As I began to wash my hair, I heard the strang-
est noise. *Clink. Clink. Clink.* I couldn't figure
out what it was. Was there something wrong
with Charlie's shower? *Clink. Clink. Clink.* I
looked down and saw glass shards falling from
my hair as I washed it. *Clink. Clink. Clink.* I
couldn't even take a normal shower.

❧

I was so tired. It seemed as if I had aged a hundred years that day. I ached all over and could
hardly keep my eyes open. But as I drifted off
to sleep, I heard the roar of a plane in the sky.
I dove under the bed and waited for impact.

After a few breathless moments, I climbed back up and tried to sleep again. Every few minutes another plane would roar past.

The F-16s patrolling the skies of Washington, D.C. didn't make me feel any safer that night. They sparked a long series of sleepless nights.

When the sun began to rise the next morning, I gratefully gave up the pretense of sleep. The aroma of coffee was already wafting through the house and it smelled like just the thing I needed. Charlie and his wife were in the kitchen and offered me a seat at the table and a cup of coffee.

"I'm heading into the office in a little bit, Dan. Do you need anything?" Charlie offered.

"No, thanks. If it's okay, I'm just going to stay here for today. I'd like to work out a way to get home. I need to see my family," I replied.

"Of course! Help yourself to anything here and if you need something you can't find, call me. There's no word yet on when airline service will resume. How are you planning to get home?" Charlie asked.

"I'll have to travel by car but I'm in no shape to drive. I'm hoping someone can come get me."

"You are welcome to be here as long as you need to be, but I hope you find a way back soon. Your family needs to see you, too," Charlie replied.

"Thanks, Charlie. I really do appreciate it."

Soon the house became quiet, except for the noise of the television. Endless news coverage showed the attacks on New York over and over again. Overhead, F-16s circled the skies in a regular pattern every fifteen minutes. Once I had identified the pattern, I no longer felt the need to take cover with every pass. But if they were early or late, I was ready to duck and run. I literally felt shaky with the endless cycle of fear and relief.

Charlie's phone rang with my parent's number on the caller ID. The phone was resting by my left side on the couch and I reached for it with my left hand. Instantly, the pain was so intense that tears came to my eyes. I reached across my lap with my right hand and tried to answer the phone calmly.

"Hello?" I answered.

"Hi, honey. How are you this morning?" my mom's concerned voice filled the space between us.

"Um, about the same, except that the shot I got in the hospital must be starting to wear off," I replied.

"Are you hurting? Didn't they give you a prescription for pain pills?" She rushed into "mom-dom" so fast I almost smiled.

"Yeah, they did, Mom. I just don't want to feel groggy until we have a plan for how I am going to get home," I told her.

"Oh! Well, good news on that. Your dad has an idea. Let me get him," she said. My dad's voice replaced my mom's.

"Dan, some of our employees are in South

Carolina on a job right now. One is going to be driving through tomorrow morning and can pick you up. He'll have you home before dinner tomorrow night." Dad's voice was in control, as always.

"Sounds good, Dad. Can you give me his cell phone number and we'll work out all the details?"

"Sure." He rattled off the number as I tried to write it legibly. "Your mom has some other messages to give you, too. See you tomorrow, son." My mom came back on the line.

"Dan? Okay, there are ten more that have called since last night and left a number for you. Do you want to do this now or wait until you get home?" Mom asked.

"Now is fine, Mom. I'm ready."

All my friends that called my cell phone heard the message that I was alive and to call my parents because I didn't want to jam up Charlie's line. They left their numbers with Mom and she relayed them to me. I was going to try to call most of them back and talk to them personally. I was really grateful that they all wanted to check on me.

Once I had hung up with Mom, I started dialing friends and reassuring them that I was okay. After just a few calls, though, I was really hurting again and decided that it was time for that pain pill and to rest.

For the next 24 hours, I alternated between phone calls, television, and trying to sleep. Even with the strong medication, sleep wouldn't come. I would tense up every time a jet flew overhead, even as I told myself that they were there for my protection. I wanted to go home where planes were on the ground and then maybe sleep could find me.

The ride home the next day was difficult. Pain was my constant companion and every bump or swerve of the car was excruciating.

Across every bridge we passed, American flags were proudly displayed. Each one reduced me to tears again.

My father's employee was kind enough to leave me mostly to myself.

In the afternoon, we turned into my parent's driveway. An American flag was draped across our front porch. The tears fell with abandon.

After 9/11, everyone understood that the American flag could work as a giant national band-aid. Firefighters hung up the flag, people hung flags from every overpass and from all of their front door stoops. It was a symbol of hope and perseverance. As we drove to my parents' house that day, September 13th, underneath bridges filled with flags, I felt the salve of national mourning and comfort. That was a true kind of patriotism I had not ever experienced before. It was powerful.

Now I have an American flag that hangs over my bed at night, and each night I sleep in comfort and security, knowing that our nation unites in times of need. In a large ceremony at the Pentagon, a huge flag was lowered over the gaping hole in the wall where the blast had occurred, and where 184 of my colleagues tragically lost their lives. It was as if the flag said, "We'll take care of our own. No matter how bad it is, we will stand tall and together."

When I came home and saw the American flag draped over the window at the front of their house, I knew that my mother and father hadn't just welcomed me home that day. They took America into their house that day; it was something much bigger. America needed a big hug that day, and the flag draped over my parents' window, the flag draped over the hole in the Pentagon, and the small flags lining the highways and streets of the country gave Americans that big hug they needed. For a few days, weeks and months, political divisions were less important, and everyone focused on healing.

It was hard to get out of the car as my left side seized up with pain but I wanted to get inside that safe place so badly that I gritted my teeth against the pain.

Mom, Dad and my brother Jim stepped out onto the porch as I worked to get out of the car. Mom reached me first. She caught me in a hug and together we cried at seeing each other. Dad and Jim also hugged me before we all headed inside together. Throughout the evening, extended family called and came over. They needed to see with their own eyes that I was okay and home and still myself. I did my best to reassure them but we all shed tears of relief at my being alive.

It's too late to find out how great somebody is, and too late to tell somebody how much you care about him or her when you are reading his or her obituary.

When I later returned to work at the Pentagon, as soon as we went through security, there were 184 obituaries up on the wall. Every single gut-wrenching day, I had to walk past those names up on the wall; reading about the heroes on the way to work. Every day I suffered under the burden of massive survivor's guilt. I should have been up on the wall with them. If I hadn't gone with Bobby on that cigarette break…

Instead of my family gathering to welcome me home, they might have been gathering to mourn my death.

But there they were, and instead of wearing black, they were wearing bright colors, tears and smiles, welcoming me back into the fold. I couldn't control my emotions either. There is no moment in life quite as powerful as the moment when you are reunited with your loved ones after such a tragedy. They were waiting at my parents' home to show their appreciation for my life, their love and support for me. They knew that I was going to be a wreck coming home.

I had cried for two days without stopping before I came home, and I had cried all the way home. And that was not something that I usually did. But this was something that I couldn't cope with, and I simply didn't know how to jettison the feelings that were inside of me. And so I wept.

Even after my emotions calmed down, and my relatives and friends began to disperse, I returned to the overwhelming flow of sadness, fear and anxiety. I remember possibly the lowest moment of my life was when I was on the couch of my parents' home, bawling my eyes out. But I overheard my father speaking with my mother, and I knew that they would help nurse me back to health.

I knew I was going to be okay physically, but emotionally; that was another matter. As I lay, weeping inconsolably on that couch, I watched in the distance as my father hugged my mother, saying, "We'll get through it, Cath, we'll get through it."

I always had my parents and my family supporting me. We all got through it together.

That day was exhausting. I hoped that with no planes flying overhead and the intense emotion I had just experienced I would finally be able to sleep that night. I immediately began to doze off, but a dog barking outside snapped me to attention. Every muscle was tense as I realized that I had been dreaming about 9/11 and the sudden noise had been an impact in my dream.

I tried to relax again. I forced myself to breathe deeply and let go of the tension that had suddenly seized up my entire body. Just as I felt drowsy, I heard a "POP!" when the front porch creaked. Again, I sat upright and looked for the point of impact. Again, I sighed and lay back down.

The cycle repeated itself countless times throughout the night.

On Friday morning, September 14th, I was laying in bed wondering when I would ever sleep again when Mom knocked on the door and said that breakfast was ready if I wanted some.

"Thanks," I said. Then I stared at my left hand, moving it side to side. *Can't feel anything, but it's moving.*

Can't control the feeling, but can control the movement, I thought to myself. *I can live with that—for now.*

I dragged myself up and winced at the pain. I made my way slowly into the kitchen as Mom was watched me closely.

"That's it," she announced. "After breakfast, I'm taking you to the ER. There must be something they can do for the pain. They are doctors after all!"

We entered the ER and asked to be seen. I walked up to the triage nurse and started to cry. I didn't know what bad news they were about to tell me, and I wasn't in a good place emotionally to receive it.

"How can I help you, sir?" he asked politely.

"I am... a... s u r v i v o r of the terrorist attack at the Pentagon," I stammered out. *Oh my God, I had just used the word "survivor"!*

"Let me get you a private room. Psych consult! ER doctor! Stat! We have a survivor of 9/11 here!" Faces snapped up and stared at me.

For what seemed like hours, doctors came by to hear my story. I told it over and over. It was their moment to connect to the pain of that day. Suddenly, the news had a face. The loss of the day had a name. My name. My face.

The doctors began a long series of treatments to ease the pain in the left side of my body. It was determined that I had absorbed the shockwave of impact with my left side.

When Mom and I got home that afternoon, I laid down. Sleep was still elusive and I listened to the phone ring repeatedly. I heard my mom answer, "Hello? Oh, hi Jane! Well, he's doing as well as we can expect. The doctors…"

"Here she goes again," I muttered. It seemed like an endless supply of family and friends had been calling to check on me. Mom gave them her standard answers and would soon hand the phone over to me so they could tell me how glad they were that I was alive and how they were sure the doctors would have me patched up in no time. I only had a couple more minutes before she would knock on the door and bring me the phone.

I couldn't do it again. I couldn't listen to their well intended platitudes and nod and smile. I couldn't sit in my parents' house and keep flashing back to a clear blue sky and the smell of jet fuel. I couldn't keep thinking every noise was another plane coming in.

I slipped out of my room and snuck toward the back door. Mom's keys were lying on the counter when I grabbed them. I scrawled a note: "Had to get out." Against doctor's orders, I got in the car and just started to drive.

I was ten years old. My cousin Brian and I were going to camp. Neither of us had ever been to this camp before but our 4-H extension agent had convinced our parents that this would be good for us. We were in the car for 45 minutes with my dad driving, Mom sitting next to him, and us in the back seat.

About ten minutes into the trip, my mom turned around to say, "Make sure you follow your counselor's directions. They know this place better than you. Do it their way." She looked so serious that I didn't dare laugh at her but I wondered if she was joking. A straight answer seemed best so I simply said, "Yes, ma'am." Mom turned back around and Brian looked at me. His eyes were narrow and he was grinning so hard that it looked like his lips would crack through with a laugh. I turned away from him to keep from laughing too, and stared out the window.

As a dairy farm came into view on my side of the car, Mom said, "It's important to try to get along with everyone you meet here." She was looking at me urgently again and I nodded and said, "Okay, Mom. I'll try." Did she think that I was going to pick fights with every kid I met? Brian was choking back giggles with a horrible fake cough. I turned to my window again as we passed the oldest gas station I had ever seen, shaking my head. Parents could be so weird!

"Make sure to eat vegetables while you are here," her voice cut into my thoughts. I closed my eyes *and gave myself a little jolt.* "What did you say, Mom?" *I asked in my most innocent voice.*

"Eat vegetables, Daniel. They are good for you!"

"Yes, Mom."

Brian was shaking with silent laughter and my cheeks were red. I am not a baby anymore, I *declared inside my head.* Don't treat me like one!

Brian slowly stopped laughing and we started talking about camp in whispers. "I wonder how many guys will be in our cabin?" *I asked.*

"Maybe we'll get to play baseball every day!" Brian exclaimed.

"I hope we—"

"Did you ask your brother to look after the cows for you? Did you tell him what time they are used to being milked?" My dad's voice interrupted me and his eyes caught mine in the rear view mirror.

"Yes, sir, I did," I replied quietly. They were my cows and I knew how to take good care of them.

Are we there yet? I wondered to myself. I focused my attention back to the world outside my window. Another dairy farm was there. Where in the world were we going? Would we ever get there?

Dad pulled the car up to the outer gates that day and drove onto the grounds. He parked the car and we all climbed out. I was glad to breathe some fresh air after that car ride.

We could smell the unique and sweet aroma of farm country. There was a farm up the road with manure issues, let's just say. But since I grew up on a farm, that smell was nothing foreign to me, and in fact, it helped me to feel right at home.

When you start walking into the camp grounds, there are wooden buildings on every side. The directors' cottage is the first one on the right. Then you walk through the camp gate. Counselors told us from the first day there that when we walked through that gate, we entered a new and exciting world, and left "reality" behind.

As a camper, this was the place where I would only be responsible for having fun! No milking cows or mucking the barn. The weight of the world always lifted off of my shoulders when I went through that gate.

Other kids complained about having to sweep up the cabin, and I would just laugh to myself. I thought, Try feeding cows at five in the morning... This is a piece of cake, guys! I mean, sleeping until seven, for crying out loud!

Automatic pilot steered me to the New London County 4-H Camp, in Franklin, Conn. I started seeing the signs on the roadway and felt the familiar surge of childhood memories.

At that moment, I didn't want to *do* anything, I just wanted to *be*. I just wanted to let go of everything. Forget about my worries. I think it was a really healthy thing to do, to go to a place where I felt secure, where I felt like I could get away from it all and hit the reset button to see what would come next.

The outer gates were locked because summer was over and kids were in school. I got out of the car, inhaled deeply, unlocked the outer gates, drove on into my haven, and left "reality" as I did as a child.

I drove up the driveway and saw the leaves beginning to change into their vibrant fall colors. I parked, got out, and walked through the second set of gates. The gravel crunched beneath my feet but that was the only sound I could hear. It was quiet here. There were no people asking what happened. No one was crying. I looked up. There were no planes flying overhead, either. I breathed in deeply again.

I climbed on top of a picnic table outside of the mess hall and sat down. Pipe cleaners from the summer's arts and crafts adventures were still scattered on the ground. The pond was in front of me, surrounded by trees bearing the colors of early fall. The wind was gentle that day; it sang its way through those leaves and my hair. When the wind was calm, the pond was as clear as glass reflecting the colors of the trees above it.

I didn't speak to anybody. I just sat there all by myself and I could only hear nature. I felt a sense of letting go.

This place was the home I had been looking for those last few days. This was the place where I needed to be. This place made sense. I felt content here even as I squeezed my left hand, hoping for the feeling to return.

I grew up in the little town of Pomfret, Connecticut.

4-H has been a part of my life since my earliest memories. When I was in kindergarten, we were learning how to tie knots and make little halters for cows. That's the earliest I can remember.

In 4-H, from the first day onwards, I felt an over-whelming sense of belonging. I felt like I belonged to something that was important. For a young kid to be part of a group that's accepting, no matter what he or she looks like or wears, that's huge. You start out with the same slate as everybody, and every-one's equal. With positive people as your leaders, you feel great about yourself and you challenge tasks as a group and you succeed.

My dad was always the leader of my 4-H club. He was always there, right from the get-go. He had also grown up in the 4-H program, so it was something that he, too, felt very passionate about, and he wanted to share it with his kids. My dad has a tremendous passion for working with children, and that's where I got it from later on.

Partially because of my dad's encouragement and support, I ended up going to the 4-H national level. As a teenager, I was running the National 4-H Congress that spent over two million dollars per year. Even as an adult, I have served on the National 4-H Leadership Trust. The 4-H organization has been a huge part of my life since the beginning.

In 1991, I first headed to Washington, D.C. with 4-H, as a delegate from the state of Connecticut, and I continued to be engaged at the national level partly because of my run-in with Miss America.

Miss America just happened to walk past me at the 1991 4-H Congress, and that can be a very formative experience for a young guy. At that day's ceremony, a fellow 4-Her was given the opportunity to introduce her from the stage, and I immediately knew what my goal would be for the next year!

I quickly leaned over to my chaperone from Connecticut and I said, "How do I get to be in one of those green jackets and get to meet Miss America?"

She said, "Well, all you've got to do is apply." Soon after I returned home, I started working on my application.

I ended up being selected, and in 1992 at the National 4-H Congress, when all of the participants were introduced, we went around the room and it finally came to me. After all of the inspirational stories that the other kids told, the moderators asked me, "Dan, why did you want to be a part of National 4-H Congress?"

I said very simply, "Look, not to disrespect anyone's story, but I'm just here to meet Miss America. So if there's a sign-up sheet, I want to sign it right now."

Everyone started laughing, thinking I was joking. I quickly corrected them, asserting: "No really, I'm serious… I'm here to meet Miss America. My greatest goal is to introduce her from the stage."

It's fun looking back and thinking about this great lesson in perseverance, because guess what... it worked.

They selected me to introduce Miss America from the stage in 1992. I had my chance to meet Miss America: Miss Leanza Cornett from the state of Florida. I got to meet her, and in front of 2,000 fellow 4-Hers, I asked for her phone number! I reached down, gave her a rose, and she gave me a kiss, and I was on Cloud Nine! And she gave me her phone number. As a side note, I actually called the number after that, just to see if it really was her phone number... and it was!

At any rate, and maybe partially because of my success in getting Miss America's number the year before, I was asked to come back in 1993 to be the co-chairman of the National 4-H Congress. Then, in 1994, I was asked to be the chairman. The group of us who were on the 1994 Congress year after year together as teenagers became lifelong friends, and we've had reunions every year since.

One of those friends even visited me in Washington around August 2001. I showed her and her family around the Pentagon.

❧·❧

About a week after 9/11, one of the kids in my 4-H club was really distraught. I talked with him because he thought I had been hurt really badly; he had seen the news report, and he had tried to stay strong, holding his emotions inside. But they all came out when he talked.

The 4-H kids are almost like my own kids. When you spend that much time together, you bond with them quickly. They're just wonderful individuals, with so much fire and everything that's great in life. Sometimes when life gets complicated, and I get a little too big for my britches, I simply go back to work with them, and they'll bring me right back down to size. Any kid will do that.

I think all of us need to work with kids when we think that we've got problems or too much on our plate. The minute you go work with children, you'll understand that they have no agenda. They have no negativity. Their purpose is to have fun, experience life, and they don't worry about everything else because it doesn't really matter.

They have always taught me that the moment I'm in right now is what really matters, and they are a great reminder. After 9/11, the kids and their worldviews amazed me. My 4-H kids helped me get through my pain and struggles.

CHAPTER FIVE

Finding Strength

HE MET MY GAZE AND FASTENED HIS *seatbelt I didn't blink as I fastened mine. He turned to look out the window. I continued to stare. Take off was bumpy but I never broke my concentration. Every muscle in my body was tense as I waited. Waited for him to make a move. Waited for him to show his intent to harm. Waited for him to flinch. My heart continued to pound and my eyes grew weary but I never stopped.*

In the fall of 2001, General Dynamics did everything in their power to ease their employees back into work at the Pentagon. The work was very stressful as we cleaned up debris in our HAZMAT suits. The rubble represented months of our work in remodeling lost; it represented lives lost.

We could no longer open our mail as the anthrax scare reached its full height. Armed guards stood at every entrance to check our security clearance.

I flew home from Washington every weekend to see my family. Touching base at home kept my spirits up and gave me something to look forward to. On one of those trips, my flight was cancelled on Friday night and I began scrambling to find another. As I searched for a different flight, I became aware of a man wearing a turban on his head. I felt chills on my arms as I watched him and felt the hair on the back of my neck rise. In a sense I blamed him for what had happened to me. In hindsight, of course that seems irrational, but in the moment, I was terrified and angry all at the same time.

Southwest had a flight with some open seats and I jumped at the chance to get home that night. As I headed over to the terminal where my flight was leaving from, I saw the man in the turban walking a few steps behind me. My heart rate increased. I reached the ticket counter and guaranteed my seat on the flight. The man in the turban waited patiently behind me and proceeded to do the same.

Now I was mad. That man had the nerve to declare his allegiance to a people and religion that had nearly killed me and now he was getting on my flight?! Well, if he *were* up to anything suspicious, I would be watching.

I placed myself behind him in the boarding line. He chose a seat that faced two other seats. I sat down right across from him and locked eyes.

45 minutes later, the plane was on the ground. I was exhausted as the man unbuckled his seatbelt and rose to his feet. Embarrassment began to creep through me. I, too, rose from my seat and stood behind him to make my

way into the aisle. I realized this guy hadn't done anything wrong. I had.

He was the one who showed bravery; wearing his religion on his sleeve. Imagine if this world were so bold that all of us could do that in our own special way, where there would be no one worrying about what other people's religions were. The world would be so peaceful if we could respect and appreciate everyone for his or her eccentricities and differences.

But here I was, staring down this man for simply wearing a turban on his head; for outwardly displaying his belief system peacefully for the entire world to see. I realized my mistake, and I felt that I needed to apologize somehow.

I had to make amends. I couldn't blame my behavior on being a victim and not take ownership for what I had done. I placed my hand on his shoulder.

"I'm sorry, sir. I had the wrong man," I said meekly.

He turned with a somber face and replied, "There has been a lot of that lately."

His gracious response to my bad behavior caused something to snap inside of me.

It was time to begin to let go. I did not want to be this person. I realized that I needed to appreciate even people of whom I was afraid. I had taken out my anger on a kind man who was probably traveling home to his family, like I was.

I was determined to set foot in the Pentagon again before my birthday on October 6th. I wanted to confront my demons and move on with my life. On September 26, 2001, I drove to the airport in Rhode Island where I would be catching a flight to Virginia.

Determination is a lousy deterrent to nervous shaking. My thoughts formed a cadence as they marched through my mind, one after another in a straight, repeating line. *The plane didn't cause 9/11. People did. I can't let fear win. I can't let them win. I can't let them win. The plane didn't cause 9/11...*

As I drove, the ring of my cell phone interrupted the chorus of those fears. My sister's voice announced that she was in labor. "You have got to be kidding me!" I told her.

I was to be the godfather of this child and I *needed* to be there. But, it had taken all of my courage to book this flight and go back. The drive to the airport had been excruciating. And now, almost there, I had to give up the ground I had gained.

We hung up and I turned the car around. I called my travel agent and asked to rebook my flight for September 30, 2001. We worked out the details and hung up. My phone rang again ten minutes after rearranging my flight. It was my sister. The contractions had stopped.

Being single and not educated in these matters, I told her, "Start them up again!"

She started to explain the details to me when I interrupted and told her, "You've got 4 days to have this baby. I just changed my flight to D.C. and I have to do this."

I drove home and waited with the rest of my family for two days. On September 28, 2001, my niece, Sydney Catherine was born. I got to be there and hold life that was so new and innocent. The experience overwhelmed me.

For all the ways that September 11th tore apart my soul, September 28th put it back together. I remember praying, "Okay God, I've nearly died this month and now I've seen new life."

I was holding a gift of new life with an arm that was still numb.

A new priority emerged and it had a tiny beating heart and big blue eyes. Her little hands were the size of my thumb and her baby-fine hair covered a perfect head. Her newborn screams would announce her arrival and her intention to rule the world of my heart. I thank God for giving me the chance to be there for that moment; to see life rise from ash.

I found the most important thing in life by turning around. Being there with family was more important than work or even healing, right then. Because for all of the healing that I knew would only be done in D.C., that moment completed my soul. I didn't know how much I would need that completion to walk through the days ahead.

On Sunday, September 30, I headed back to the airport. The drive back was familiarly anxious. Again, my cadence of thought kept time with the tires as I talked myself into getting on a plane. Once I was in the terminal, I knew that if I was going to get on that flight, I could use some help. A very large margarita was just the right medication to see me through! I even managed to be relaxed enough to get the flight attendant laughing, too.

When the plane was safely on the ground in D.C., I called my parents and told them, "Okay, part one is taken care of."

I unlocked the door to my apartment after being gone for almost a month. When I walked in, it was September 11th again. There was my green ribbon from triage sitting on my dresser. My clothes, stained with soot and blood, sat on the bed. The smell of pulverized cement filled my nostrils. I fell to the floor and cried. There were seriously injured people all around me. Jet fuel and black smoke were thick in the air. There was a fireball. There was a collapsing building. There were screams. There was another plane coming to hit us. The horror playing out in my mind wouldn't stop.

I couldn't have foreseen this part of the recovery after leaving the safety of my parent's home. It hit me like a ton of bricks that I was part of America's largest terrorist attack on our soil as a survivor. As I lay there on the floor, my left side was still numb from the blast and I flexed my left hand repeatedly to make sure that I could still move it.

On Monday, I went back to work for the first time at our offices in Virginia. Bobby and I exchanged recovery stories and were relieved to find similarities. We had both been suffering from tremendous headaches but there was a sense of being normal if both of us were experiencing them.

On Tuesday, October 2, I went back into the Pentagon. There were armed guards at the doors and makeshift memorials everywhere. We were required to wear hazmat suits and respirators. Suiting up with a numb left side took some time. I was shaking and exhausted by the time I was finished.

I asked my teammates to show me where we had been on that Tuesday, September 11th morning. They led me slowly to a pile of rubble. There was nothing of that corridor left. The collapse had taken it all. I instantly wondered what had happened to the guys in the office we were heading to that day.

"What happened to the guys in the naval command center?" I asked.

No one answered at first. I pushed hard for a response. Finally, Bobby told me, "No one made it out."

A tsunami drowned me. The overriding theme was that I should have died, too. Wave after wave crashed into me filling my mouth with water. I was only alive because of a cigarette break. I didn't know if that was terrible or lucky. I knew some of the people in that office. I had worked in and out of there for weeks. They were wonderful people who didn't get to say goodbye to their families. They didn't choose to die. They were true heroes who gave their everyday lives to protecting America. They would never see their children play baseball again. They would never travel to a new place again. They would never kiss their spouses goodnight again. I should have been one of them; *what right did I have to survive? Why did I get to see my niece born when they would never have another day with their children?*

That was one of my lowest points. I lost any will or desire to live. The weight of the guilt suffocated me. No one could logically understand a plane hitting a building. The whole nation was shocked and sorrowful but I grieved personally. I knew those people's faces; they were my colleagues. I had seen pictures of their families on their desks. I had heard them chat over their morning coffee. I should have been with them.

The world went from gray to black.

Sunday morning dawned crisp as I watched the sunrise. Fatigue was a familiar feeling by now and I rose from another sleepless night to find my mom in the kitchen.

"Dan, it's Sunday and we are going to church. Go get dressed," she ordered.

I could have been ten years old all over again. The thought made me smile and I went to obey. Nobody messes with Mom when it is time to get to church.

Mass was familiar, beautiful, and comforting. I found myself soothed by words that I had been hearing since I was a child and felt secure. In that safe place, I formed words around the question that had been lingering since Tuesday.

"How could this happen, God?" I asked Him.

The question surfaced with such force that I found tears on my face and my heart pounding.

"How could this happen, God?"

I continued with my eyes shut tightly: "I thought You were in control, God? How could this have happened? Why didn't you stop it? Where is Your control, God? Why did I live? Why am I still here?"

The questions overwhelmed me and my responses to the service were silent.

After the service was over, friends and family surrounded me to offer comfort. Their concern was welcome and I felt consoled.

The days after that blur together.

Nightmares, tears, insomnia, pain, physical therapy, questions, guilt…

I began to learn to live with them all. Not thrive and not really heal, but survive.

The strongest foundation in my life has always been my religion. When everything else in the world shook on 9/11, that was the one thing that didn't.

When I went to church that first time I absolutely lost it because it was when I realized that my foundation was surrounding me, and I could just let it all go. I could let all the pain that I experienced, all the anxiety, all the fears and everything go, and I cried during that service.

At the very end, the whole church came around and gave me a hug after that. It confirmed that my foundation in life very much is my religion, and my foundation held up strong that day.

There are two avenues to that. One is the power of prayer, and that prayer itself is essentially its people. It can be from any religion, but it is the people who are extending their hearts to you when they pray for you. It's people who really take the gifts that they have from within and put it out on their sleeve for the betterment of others.

I've always believed that God won't put anything on your plate that you can't handle. Having those people surround me was just saying let me take a portion of that off your plate and we'll get through it together. God needed to know that this was too much on my plate.

One of my many trips to Connecticut in the fall of 2001 was for a long weekend celebrating Thanksgiving. I flew home on Wednesday afternoon, looking forward to the next day.

I am from a large family. On Thanksgiving, about 75 of us come together to celebrate. It's a large, loud, and really fun time. We rent out the local firehouse so that we have room for everyone. The children play games while the women chat about who made what this year. The men watch football before dinner. Conversation is funny and casual. I was looking forward to a chance to blend in somewhere and feel normal.

Mom, Dad and I arrived later than we had planned—which is part of every Thanksgiving experience. I found myself actually wanting to smile at memories of Thanksgivings past. All three of us were carrying food so that we could make it in with just one trip. The weather had turned really cold, so everyone was inside the firehouse, even the kids. As Dad fumbled with the door, I could hear the buzz of voices inside. Someone laughed out loud.

When Dad managed the door and we all walked through, it felt like someone had stopped time. Conversation froze and so did each and every person. The freeze only lasted a moment but I felt every eye on me as I walked with Mom and Dad to the huge table.

Immediately, a pit in my stomach opened up and I wondered where all the darkness had been stored just moments ago. Waves of fear, panic and grief came over me and I fought back tears. I felt my left arm begin to throb and I stooped my shoulders a bit to ease the pain.

As I turned around, hoping no one was watching, my Aunt Jane called everyone to attention. Thankfully, all eyes went to her and I tried to breathe deeply.

"We are going to try something new this year. I have a quilt ready for us with a square for each person represented here. You are to choose one square and write what you are thankful for. You only get one and yes, everyone has to do it! At the end of the day, we'll look over it together. Dinner is in half an hour."

A line began to form around the quilt with a low buzz of conversation.

"What are you going to write?"

"Do you know what you will put?"

"Do you think Aunt Jane will count? What if someone doesn't do it?"

"Yes, Aunt Jane will count. And yes, she'll know who didn't do it."

They were right. Aunt Jane required 110% participation in her projects.

What was I thankful for? Being alive? Yes, but what about all those who weren't?

Thankful for my family? Yes, but what about all those families that were missing someone at the table today?

Thankful for freedom? Yes, but at what cost?

Thankful?

My thoughts were bouncing around when my sister, Amy, linked her arm through mine.

She had Sydney with her. The tiny little blob had grown into a baby in the last two months. Her sweet face was relaxed as she slept in her mother's arms. Thankful. Yes, I could be thankful for Sydney, with no strings attached. I managed a weak smile for Amy and took Sydney from her.

Later that evening, back at Mom and Dad's house, I was holding Sydney again when Amy asked in a low voice, "Dan, are you sleeping at all? You look terrible."

"Gee, thanks," I replied. "No, I can't sleep. I fall asleep but wake up with every noise having the same nightmare over and over."

"Dan, I'm worried about you. Maybe you need to see another doctor. Maybe you need to think about some therapy." It was only the genuine concern on her face that stopped me from ignoring her completely.

"Amy, doctors don't know what to do with me either. Remember the ER? I don't want to go tell my story to some other doctor just to hear that they don't know what to do."

She let it go at that but I knew she wasn't the only one worried.

Just a few short weeks later I was home again. This time, I was home for a week to celebrate Christmas. I had no anticipation or joy at the thought of Christmas approaching. My nightmares now included children's faces that I didn't recognize. I would wake up and focus on those faces. I would wonder whose child it was and if they still had a parent.

I tried to get excited about the holiday for the sake of Brendan, my nephew. He was two and looking forward to presents. I bought him a Boston Red Sox jersey and planned to take him to a game in the spring. But, I couldn't even get excited about the sport and team I had loved so much.

My dad had been in and out the hospital for the last couple of weeks. He kept having chest pain and doctors told him to cut out the stress. I knew some of it was about me.

One night, Dad and I were the only ones still up. The house was dark except for the lights of the Christmas tree. We sat in the living room staring at it, neither one of us speaking for a long time. Finally Dad broke the silence.

"Dan, I need a favor."

"Sure, Dad. What do you need?"

"I need you to help me run the business."

"What?" I was sure that I hadn't heard him correctly.

"I need you to help me run the business. You are a manager and we need that."

"Dad, I work at the Pentagon. I make lots of money working with people I really like. I am doing a job that I love and they fly me home to see the Red Sox play. You want me to give that up to come work in the family electrical business?"

"Yes. I need your help. I can't take care of everything that needs to be done. The doctors are on me to work less and I need someone that I trust to handle things. I trust you."

"Dad, are you serious? Is this just a way to get me away from Washington, D.C.... . So I'll be safe?"

"Dan, really. I need your help with the business. You'd be VP of operations."

"Okay, but I need some time to think about it."

The next week was filled with kids, family and presents. I tried to truly be present and engage with what was happening, but it was a real challenge. I was still jumpy. I couldn't sleep. And now, I was wrestling with this new decision. I knew that family was the top of my priority list but caving in to fear was not acceptable. If I played it safe, the terrorists would have won. They would have left me living my life in fear. I would not allow that! But, Dad said that he really did need my help. How could I turn him down?

I loved D.C. and I loved working there. My co-workers had become another kind of family to me. They were my family by choice. We made a great team for work but we also enjoyed being together outside of work. Bobby would goofily come in and say that he had a "kitchen pass" from his wife to go out after work. We would all laugh together over drinks and dinner. Being together was a real joy.

But, January 2, 2002 found me in the office of my manager giving my two-week notice.

It tore me up to leave General Dynamics. I had given so much to them and had loved my work. Tom Buonforte, my manager, assured me that I had made the right decision to support my family at this time.

News spread like wildfire that I was leaving. Before the day was out, I had calls from all over the country as friends and former co-workers checked to see if it was true. I spent those last two weeks in D.C. enjoying these wonderful people that I had come to call family.

On my last day, I asked my colleagues to sign a pencil drawing of the Pentagon. Each signed a short sentiment with their name, but Bobby summed it all up.

"Come back and have a smoke with me!" he wrote.

I began working as the vice president of operations at Eagle Electric on January 22, 2002.

I was searching for something normal and so I went out on a date, the first one since 9/11. I had been interested in this girl for a long time and decided that it was time to try to find good, positive things in my life. I had the normal, first date jitters but thought this could go really well.

We were eating dinner out when someone on the floor below us slammed a door. The sound was piercing to me and I dashed under the table. Then I heard a small voice asking, "Are you okay down there?"

"Look! The asparagus I was missing!" I joked back, my sense of humor taking over.

She asked me to tell her about 9/11 and then I would never have to talk about it again. I did.

Even a new job and a first date couldn't over-shadow the grief and guilt that was consuming me. The nightmares became more vivid. The sense of shame at having survived weighed me down. I wondered if there was an end or if the rest of my life would look like this.

CHAPTER SIX

Reaching Out

MY ALARM BLARED.

I slammed my fist on the snooze button. There was never really any need to set the alarm. I was always awake when it sounded, but I set it every night anyway, hoping that that would be the night I would actually sleep.

It was Memorial Day. Like every other Memorial Day, our 4-H club was going to march in our town's parade. My 4-H kids and I would go to the town garage, get the float, and move it on to the parade route. The parade would start slowly, and late. We would walk through the downtown square as we waved to all the people. And, like every other year, I was sure that it would rain. Our hometown parade just wasn't a parade without it raining. Our standard 4-H khaki pants and white shirts would be spattered with mud, again.

After the parade, all of my family would head out to the farm for a huge lunch. Memorial Day was more than a tradition around here; it was comforting and predictable.

My alarm went off again. It was time to get up for real. My eyes lingered on the large flag hanging on my wall. I had displayed it for years, but it had taken on special meaning in the last 8 months. The stripes were bold in color, and each of those 50 stars was home to someone. This wasn't just any Memorial Day.

My tears started in the shower. I had learned to just let myself cry when another wave of sobbing overtook me. Faces of colleagues in the triage area paraded through my mind's eye. After several minutes of sobbing to myself, I felt like control was close and I started getting ready.

I drove to my parent's house to ride with Dad to pick up the float. Dad always drove the truck that pulled our 4-H float. This year my nephew, Brendan, barely two years old, was going to ride with him. I met my dad as they were stepping out of the house. I tried to muster up a smile for Brendan, but it fell flat.

We walked to the truck and buckled Brendan into his car seat. I walked around and climbed into the front as Dad started the car. Brendan was already chattering his happy toddler language in the back when Dad said, "Dan, are you okay? You seem quiet this morning."

"Today's going to be really hard." I muttered. "I'm not sure how I'm going to handle it all."

"Well, son," he replied, "we'll just do the best we can."

Some of my 4-H kids were already at the garage, getting ready to put the finishing touches on our red barn float. Working with

4-H had been a tool for survival these last eight months. These kids gave me energy. It seemed that they shared their overabundance of it without meaning to.

"Hi Dan! Look, I added on to the barn here. What do you think?"

"Hey Dan! Who's the little guy in the truck?"

"Dan! My mom said we could have a summer swim party at our house for the 4-H club. Is that okay with you?"

Happy voices and smiling faces seemed out of place to me, but they had worked so hard to make our float look great. I forced a smile. "Good morning! This is my nephew, Brendan; and everyone knows my dad, Mr. Holdridge. The float looks amazing. Way to go, everybody!"

We carefully hitched the trailer to Dad's truck and made our way to our assigned spot in the parade route. The kids and I walked behind Dad and Brendan in the truck. We still had a few minutes before things got underway, but most of the parade was assembled. Maybe we would actually start on time this year.

We walked past fire trucks, complete with uniformed firefighters who gave a quick "whoop" on the siren to acknowledge us as we went by. The police department was there as well, with patrol cars displaying flags in the windows. Local Boy and Girl Scout troops were lining up and my kids called out to their friends. Somewhere nearby, the high school band was warming up. At the end of the line were the horses, already skittish from the noise. Overhead, the sky was thick with clouds, making everything seem dreary.

Dad maneuvered the truck into our spot between another 4-H club's tractor float and the Garden Club. My kids immediately began comparing their float to the other 4-H clubs' floats. The Garden Club had created a beautiful float covered in fresh flowers, but they were beginning to droop from the exhaust of the truck that was pulling it.

I tried to involve myself with my kids around me, engaging them in conversations about school and their 4-H projects. I'm not sure what words came out of my mouth but it was better than giving in to the tears again. I looked through the back window of Dad's truck to see him and Brendan chattering together. Dad was laughing at something Brendan had said and Brendan was looking pleased with himself at having made his grandfather laugh so hard. Brendan caught me looking at him and waved a tiny, plastic American flag through the window. I choked back tears.

A loud bang stopped me from letting those tears loose. Our local Army National Guard had begun the parade with a gun salute and I had to stop myself from seeking shelter. Eight months had passed and loud noises still left me unnerved. At a speed of less than 5 miles per hour, we trudged toward downtown. My nerves were frayed.

North Stonington, Connecticut, is a typical New England town. The town hall is a

small brick building that would be displaying a flag on that day. All the buildings are
historic and the traffic circle is lined with
red brick. It was also lined with people, lots
of people, that day. I dreaded all those eyes
looking at me and knowing what I had been
through, recognizing the agony of today for
me. I would have marched away if I could
have but instead, the flow of the parade was
leading us toward the inevitable.

We walked for several blocks before we saw
anyone lining the street. At first the crowd
seemed sparse compared to years past. Then a
resounding cheer went up and I knew that the
National Guard had reached the downtown
square. The cheering grew as we approached
and I wondered why the spectators were so
loud today.

The sky was still threatening rain but so far
had held off. The air was thick with humidity and my shirt felt damp from it. Dad
glanced over his shoulder to check on me
and the float. I gave him a thumbs up with
a forced smile.

Dad's truck was rounding the intersection that heralded the entrance to downtown when I caught my first glimpse of the throngs of people. The faces were indistinguishable and the crowd seemed to be several yards deep on every street, sidewalk, and grassy opening of downtown. Every one of them had an American flag. The colors saturated my eyes as their yelling filled my ears. I didn't know this many people lived in North Stonington, much less came to the parade. Their excitement made the air feel electric, and the atmosphere felt like a major league baseball game, rather than a hometown Memorial Day parade.

Every other Memorial Day had been about men and women far removed from me. They fought in wars before I was born, in places I couldn't pronounce. They were mostly old men who wore hats and jackets with lots of pins. They deserved my respect, but were nameless faces to me. I have always been grateful to be an American and aware that sacrifice had created that opportunity for me, but I didn't personally know anyone who had sacrificed.

But today I could picture people that I knew; people who died in the building where I worked. People I had seen in the Pentagon courtyard every day. People who had relied on me to fix their computers so they could do their jobs. Today, I saw *their* faces.

The sight of all those flags waving, in the hands of old and young alike, was more than I could take in. Part of me wanted them to stop; part of me felt supported by the gesture.

Ever since 9/11, people seemed to see me as a veteran in some strange way since I worked in a military location. But I didn't intend to be on a battlefield that day. I just went to work. Somehow, by some horrible twist of fate, I was a survivor of a war that I wandered into by accident. Today, those flags were for me. But I hadn't earned them. I didn't enlist or go away for training. I just went to work. I just rode an elevator and stopped with a friend for a cigarette break. I didn't deserve those flags. I was stealing someone else's honor.

The people waving flags had suffered, too. They had felt the losses. "We are in this together," their flags said. Part of me mourned for my colleagues who weren't here to see this. I wondered if their children marched in a parade somewhere today, or if people were waving flags for them.

As I tried to adjust to the swell of the crowd, I caught sight of a true veteran. He was wearing a Navy insignia on his jacket with medals and pins. He, too, held a small flag in his hand but his arm was limp by his side. Under his baseball cap that bore our local VA chapter symbol, tears ran down his face. Our eyes locked as I came to the place where he stood.

I could hardly keep my feet moving. The kids around me disappeared. The sounds were muted. The colors dulled. In a monumental effort, I dragged one foot after the other in order to avoid being run over by the Garden club. There was no bottom to the pit that I was in. The tears were salty on my lips and there wasn't even any rain to disguise them.

It was only the years of experience in this parade that moved me to the end of our route. My mind couldn't process anything but grief. Parents were waiting there to pick up their children, but I could no longer be responsible for anyone but myself. I should go back to where my family was standing. I should go back to that veteran and shake his hand. I should ride back to my parents' house for lunch. I should go scoop up Brendan and tell him how great he did in the parade. I should...but I couldn't.

All I could do was cry. I stood alone behind the town firehouse as waves of grief and confusion crashed in again.

Why did it happen? Why did I live? Why did so many have to die?

The tears fell to the grass beneath my feet and I couldn't hide or stop them. Sobs began to build and my entire body shook from the force of them.

Why did I live? Why did they die? Why was I here? Why was I spared?

A hand on my shoulder startled me. I looked up into my dad's face. He understood without saying a word and I sobbed.

"I can't come to lunch, Dad," I sputtered out after a long silence.

"That's okay," he said. "What will you do?"

"I don't know, but I need some time."

When the sobs let up and I insisted that I needed to be alone, Dad went home to handle the family. Home wasn't that far, but I drove a while to get there.

The sky was still dark and casting a depressing shadow on everything I saw. Life was heavy, painful, and slow. I hadn't slept in months. I only ate when my mom was around to fuss. There was no real joy to be found. Sure, my nephew and niece were cute. Yes, I was working hard with Dad and facing a new chapter in my career, but I had no spark. I carried the weight of 184 people who were dead and I felt like I should have been number 185. I wandered towards home.

I finally walked through my door, well after sunset. Thunder had been rumbling in the distance and it seemed best to get home before the storm that had been brewing all day broke. I pulled out my cell phone. I knew what was next. But I wasn't sure I had the courage to face it. I put my phone down again.

Outside the deluge of rain and hail began. The storm lasted through the night with flash flooding and high winds. Tree branches were torn off and thrown around. Roofs were damaged and windows broken. Tiny summer buds were ripped from their stems and tender green leaves thrashed from tree limbs. I watched the damage occur all night long. I stared sleeplessly out the window.

Dawn crept in the next day, and then, my alarm blared.

It was time. I turned off the alarm.

I reached for my cell phone and called my brother-in-law. I stared at the flag on the wall. I inhaled deeply. I slowly exhaled.

"Hello?"

"Hi, Darin. It's Dan. I think it's time. Will you give me the name of that therapist again?"

◆⋈◆

Healing is a very slow process when you're healing the heart. But no matter how bad the situation, things will get better.

Patience is the key.

There are no easy answers.

There's no one solution.

One day at a time. I decided to go in for counseling that day because everything became too overwhelming. I carried the weight of the world around on my shoulders.

That day was the first day I asked for help, and it was the beginning of my true recovery, surrounded by doctors, family and friends. I can never repay the gifts they have given me in my times of need.

PART III

CHAPTER SEVEN

What Matters Most

A WEEK LATER, I WAS TAKING MY DOGS FOR a walk after work one night when I realized that summer wouldn't be around much longer. It was already beginning to turn rainy and cool. Here and there, a single leaf on a tree was beginning to change color. Fall was almost here.

September 11th would be here before I knew it. It had been almost a year. *A year? Could that be right?* Some nights the nightmares were so vivid that it felt like September 11, 2001 had repeated itself over and over for almost a year. At the same time, so much had changed. I was living in Connecticut now and running the family's business. Sydney's first birthday was fast approaching. Life had continued; but had I?

How do you heal from such a moment? One thought had been circling in my head for weeks now and it was time to give it words.

"I have to forgive them, Big Papi," I told my dog. "I have to let go of my anger and hatred for the terrorists. It is eating me up inside and keeping me from moving on. I have to forgive them. If I can do it, they lose their power over me. If I can let go of this anger, I can regain control. I'm going to try."

I looked up at the sunset and took a deep breath.

I had been seeing my therapist for almost two months now. Under his care, I had begun to sleep again. With his instruction, I was exercising regularly and trying to eat well. Therapy wasn't entirely what I had expected.

While we did talk about 9/11, we spent a lot of time talking about life and how I thought.

The end of our last session was still haunting me. We were talking about all of the volunteer work I had done and am still involved in. He had me calculate the number of hours I had volunteered last year. It came to over three thousand. John simply asked me, "Why? Why do you live your life for everybody but you?"

I got mad when he said it because I was doing something worthwhile with my life. I was giving of myself to others and working to build a better world and invest myself in kids. Shouldn't I be living my life to help other people?

But all week, that question has bothered me. Why, indeed? Why do I do so many hours of volunteer work? Is it possible that my volunteerism is more about me than the ones I serve? Am I supposed to live this way?

So, I was trying to keep the hours spent on volunteer projects in check this week. It was an experiment to see what if felt like. I certainly felt less stressed out. I had time to work out everyday and play with my dogs at night. But I was also aware that I felt like something was missing. I just couldn't name it yet. Volunteering so much gave me something; I needed to know what it was.

"I want to forgive. I want to release hatred and anger. I want to forgive the men that brought about that awful day. Those terrorists had no business doing what they did: getting on planes and planning to kill people. It is just so inhumane. It is so sad when people could have enough hatred that they would attempt to take the lives of innocent people. But I won't let that same kind of hate live in me towards them. I want to forgive."

I didn't feel magically different on the way back to my house. But I knew that something could begin to change if I kept reminding myself not to hate.

The step back from volunteering was just as hard. It had been two weeks of stopping myself from jumping into every situation at the 4-H camp. It had been two weeks of knowing who was calling and knowing that I could help, but making a decision to wait. It was exhausting! More than that, I was feeling really guilty. I was letting them down, failing them. They knew that I was the best person to call and so I should have been helping them when they asked. Instead, I hid behind my cell phone and email.

However, it wasn't like camp was falling apart. The kids seemed to be having fun and the director was holding his own. Licensing had just been renewed after a great inspection. The camp was doing fine but I wanted it to succeed with my help.

There it was again. It was about me. More than once in the last two weeks, I had caught myself thinking this way. I needed the acceptance because I always felt great helping others. Kind of a euphoria, a drug, it felt so good to give. Could somebody be addicted to the spirit of giving?

I thought back to my last therapy session and could picture the conversation:

"Think about two concentric circles, Dan. One is larger than the other. The outer circle is what others see about you. It is their opinion and experience with you. The inner circle is you: what you think and feel and why you are yourself. There is power in that inner circle. It is power of knowing yourself. Our lives have to exist in both of these circles. It is a balancing act to live in them both in healthy ways. Where do you live most of your life?"

I had known the answer immediately but I didn't want to say it out loud. I was living my life for everyone else. I was more concerned about what everyone thought of me rather than what I thought of myself. I just thought that life was about trying to help others and make other people happy. I looked happy but I didn't really have a purpose. I knew that I had lived my life completely in the outer circle without regard for the inner.

The truth was that I didn't know what the inner circle even looked like. How could I find power in knowing myself? What did that even mean?

We were back to the house now and Big Papi was ready for some dinner. My mind was still racing around as I thought about the circle. I needed something specific to apply it to. Had I moved back to Connecticut only to please my dad? Was it only to help him out or was there an element of something for me in it?

I had been so focused on going back to D.C. and not letting terror win. That was still the right idea, I was sure, but living it out was so hard. I was working with guns pointed at me. I walked past the obituaries of all the people who died right there. Anthrax kept me from being able to open my mail. Maybe my decision was not only to help my family out but in actuality to help me, too. It was what I really wanted and Dad had given me a good reason to do it.

What else did I really want? What did I really

want to do that I had never done before? I want to go the Baseball Hall of Fame. I want to go to Europe. I want to find a meaningful way to share what happened to me on 9/11.

Was it okay to want those things? Why had I never done them before? The answer was, I had never taken the time. I was always busy with 4-H kids and the camp and I never stopped to do something that I loved and wanted to do. I did love working with 4-H but maybe I loved it as much because of how it made me feel.

What would a life lived from that inner circle look like?

CHAPTER EIGHT

The Energy of Healing

I SETTLED INTO MY SEAT AND TURNED OFF my cell phone. My window seat afforded me a view of luggage being loaded into the underbelly of our plane.

The envelope in my pocket scratched me as I fastened my seat belt. I pulled it out and then secured the belt around my waist. The pages inside were worn by now. I had read this letter dozens of times.

Dear Mr. Holdridge,

On behalf of the Topeka Baptist Church, in Jayess,

Mississippi, I am honored to let you know that we spent an evening in prayer on your behalf. We understand that you were injured on September 11, 2001 and we prayed for your recovery. Please find attached a list of those who prayed for you.

The next page was a sea of names and well wishes and blessings.

This was the whole reason I was on this plane. This simple letter had me flying away from my family on the day before Thanksgiving. I let my mind wander as we took off.

In October 2001, the depth of survivor's guilt was a dark, unforgiving forest. I was unable to shake the idea that so many had died while I had survived. I dwelled on the loss of their spouses and children. I would wonder who was cheering those kids on at soccer games and dance recitals. Who was helping them with math homework and who drove them to school? Can children bounce back after having their parents die without saying goodbye? What about the parents whose children had been on that airplane? How do you grieve for your child? How do you find hope in the future?

Why didn't I die too? How did I earn the chance to live? I didn't have any kids to miss me. I didn't have a wife waiting for me. Why was I alive?

I went to work every morning at the Pentagon through armed guards who checked every ID twice while holding rifles. I moved past security into the "Hall of Honor" that held the obituaries of each Pentagon employee who had died. The hall was full of flags, pictures of the deceased, and tokens of sympathy from around the nation. It was like walking into pain, pain that had a face and was its own presence in the room. I would move like a ghost through that hall, afraid that one of the mourners would look at me and ask, "Why aren't you here, too?"

I wore a coat made of grief and guilt all the time.

After every long day, I was forced to walk past those security guards and their rifles again. I would drive my car back to the apartment building where I lived. The elevator was just past the mailboxes so I would grab the envelopes from my box to sort through on the ride up to my apartment.

One day, there was an envelope from a church in Mississippi. I expected a fundraising letter of some kind, so I tucked it into the back of the pile. I found my cell phone bill and an advertisement for a local market before the doors opened on my floor. I unlocked and opened the door while juggling the mail and my backpack.

In the kitchen, I opened the cell phone bill and threw away the ad. The church address caught my attention again. This time I opened it.

Now here I was, two years later, riding a plane to Jackson, Mississippi. My friend Shelley, who attends the Topeka Baptist Church, was waiting in the airport for me. I would spend Thanksgiving with her family, and then on Sunday morning, I would get up and thank the church for praying for me.

I had spoken to some groups about 9/11 before. I mainly told them what had happened to me that day and encouraged them to appreciate the lives they had been given. It was a painful exercise for me. Whenever I spoke about it, the screams and the smell of jet fuel became real again. Whenever I finished one of those speeches, I would be shaking and desperate to sleep. My left arm would throb again, and it would take hours to recover.

I had the sense that speaking to this group would be a little different. I wasn't just going to tell them my story, I wanted to thank them. They had offered me a reason to push back against my awful thoughts. They had shown me light after the darkness of depression.

But still, I dreaded doing this. Reliving that day was debilitating, but I had a sense of duty about it. I felt required to speak this message.

The pace of life in Mississippi is different than in Connecticut. Traffic moves slower. People move slower. They even talk slower. Slower is welcome! I felt my lungs fill

completely, and I couldn't resist the sigh that
escaped in the exhale. I wondered if Shelley
knew she lived in a restful place, or if she
was too used to it.

I slept deeply on Wednesday night in a
charming room in Shelley's parents' house.
On Thursday, all of Shelley's family came to
Thanksgiving dinner.

They were warm people who were easy to be
with. They welcomed me into their family
for this holiday. Mr. Smith, Shelley's dad, was
in his early fifties with graying hair that all
his children teased about being combed over
the top of his nearly bald head. His cowboy
boots at the dinner table surprised me, but no
one else even noticed.

Mrs. Smith was the epitome of a Southern
woman. Her clothes were perfectly matched
to the dinner table and she wore a string of
pearls around her neck. She offered dinner to
each of her children, their spouses, and me
as a gift of love. Her sandy blonde hair and
youthful smile made her age difficult to guess.

It was easy to tell that Shelley, her older sister, and her younger brother were all related. They had the same smile as their mother, and their father's sense of humor. Angela, the oldest, and her husband sat across the table from me. Shelley sat between me and her husband. Shelley's little brother, Justin, had just gotten engaged and his fiancé was enjoying her first Thanksgiving with the family.

The nine of us gathered around a dining room table full of delicious smelling food. It seemed natural when we joined hands and Shelley's father spoke a prayer of thankfulness. The depth of my thanks that day ran deep. I was thankful for my family, and my job, and for these kind people I was with. And finally, I was able to be thankful for having survived two years ago.

"Mom! These sweet potatoes are wonderful! How much butter did you put in them?" Angela, Shelley's older sister, asked teasingly. Every one else laughed out loud and Shelley leaned over to me.

"Mom cooks like real Southerner's do: butter is the secret ingredient to everything on the table. That's why we are all shaped this way!" she told me.

The easy laughter and gentleness of these people made me feel at home.

Friday and Saturday were spent relaxing in rural Mississippi. Justin and Mr. Smith showed me how to fish with a two liter bottle in the pond. Mrs. Smith plied me with buttery food all weekend and smiled so sweetly that I couldn't say no.

But underneath it all ran a current of anxiety. Sunday was coming. I was here for a purpose beyond enjoying this nice family. On Saturday afternoon, I pulled Shelley aside.

"I need to go over this speech again. I made some changes on the flight here. Will you look it over for me?" I asked.

"Dan, you've rewritten this speech 20 times. You're going to do great. You're prepared.

You don't need me to edit it again," she said, sternly. Her face softened and she said, "I will look at it if it makes you feel better, but you've got to relax."

"I just don't think I've said it right. I need to tell them how important that letter was to me, and I need to connect with them. I just don't think I've got it right yet," I worried.

"Okay, let's look at it again," she agreed.

Hours later she told me to stop obsessing and get some sleep. She went home and I tried to relax.

Sunday dawned bright and clear. It looked warm for November, but beautiful. The trees were brilliant colors of scarlet and gold. I was glad for my suit coat as we walked outside that morning into a gust of wind. Mr. Smith walked beside me to the car in his suit and cowboy boots.

I was regretting the coffee and buttery toast that I had forced down out of politeness.

I rode with Shelley and her parents to the Topeka Baptist Church. The drive was really short through picturesque rural Mississippi. The church itself was a brick building with a white steeple. It seemed large for the neighborhood we had just been in. I wondered if they actually filled the building.

Shelley's dad pulled into the parking lot on the side of the building. We were among the first to arrive, with only a few other cars in the lot. The side of the building that we were facing was dotted with windows that reflected the blinding morning sun. We stepped up onto the covered porch area and pulled open the white double doors.

The sanctuary was visible from where we entered and we could hear a few members of the choir beginning to warm up. Shelley walked up to a tall man and turned to me.

"Dan, this is Brother Dale, our pastor. He's going to handle the details with you this morning. I need to go warm up."

"Nice to meet you, Brother Dale. I'm fine, Shelley. Go ahead," I replied.

Brother Dale's accent was different than Shelley's, and thick. His salt and pepper hair stood in contrast to his dark olive skin. His white button down shirt was starched to perfection under his navy suit. His eyes seemed to be laughing as he looked at me.

Shelley started playing the piano for the choir and Brother Dale motioned for me to follow him. The toast was churning in my stomach as we walked through the sanctuary.

The floors were covered in teal colored carpet that met dark, wood-paneled walls. Light was streaming into the room through the windows I had seen outside. The vaulted ceiling that formed the steeple was white, and reflected the sunlight. Brother Dale walked up the aisle on the right side of the room and opened a door to a little office at the front.

"This is my Sunday office," he said, his voice echoing in that little room. "I like to hear the choir warming up as I get ready to preach."

I nodded and said, "They sound great." I sounded nervous, even to myself. I needed to calm down.

"What are you going to talk about?" Brother Dale asked, smiling.

"I plan to speak about the power and gift of prayer that this church offered me. I want to tell them thank you. I have it all here," I said as I pulled out my manuscript.

Brother Dale nodded and said, "That will be just right. Shelley has prepared a special solo for today and then I will get up and introduce you. The microphone on the pulpit is a little tricky. Make sure and lean into it."

I thanked him and turned to walk back into the sanctuary.

"Dan!" Brother Dale called.

"Yes?" I asked, turning back to face him. He placed his hands on my shoulders and looked at me intently.

"Let God speak through you," Dale said.

I nodded slowly and he let go. I turned and walked into the sanctuary wondering, *Is that a Southern Baptist thing? What does that mean?*

I put it from my mind and sat down close to the front of the room. Shelley was playing some pretty music as people came in. It seemed like every one of them was smiling and hugging their friends as they found a seat. I was amazed that every seat was full.

Service began when the choir started singing along with the piano. They were wonderful. Someone got up to pray and then Shelley stepped out from behind the piano. She sang the most beautiful solo. Her voice soared to that steeple and wrapped around the people, too. Words about being driven to pray and finding power when you are praying jumped out at me and helped dry the sweat on my hands. It was one of those moments that make you want to close your eyes and record the emotion in your mind, so it will never leave you.

After Shelley's solo, Brother Dale got up to introduce me. He told the church that I was there to give my testimony. I wasn't sure what that meant but I hoped that my speech fit that category.

I walked up to the large wooden podium and looked out on those kind faces. And then something surprising happened. I don't know if it was Shelley's solo or Brother Dale's statement before church, but something told me to leave my slaved-over speech inside the hollow back of the podium, and just talk.

I kept staring at that crowd for what seemed too long, but was really only a second. I closed my eyes and took a deep breath. And then, I did it. I folded the pages together and put them away.

Words began to pour out—words that I had prepared and some that I had not. I told them about what had happened to me on 9/11 and about the hopeless state I had been in. I told them about wondering why I had lived. I told them about getting their letter and how God had arranged for it to arrive at my darkest hour. I told them that it closed the door on the awful thoughts that had begun to haunt me; that prayer had saved my life, not just on September 11th, but in October, and in November, and through the next year, and even now. I told them that God had used their prayers to save me.

"Thank you," I said. "Your gift of prayer saved my life, for the second time. Your gift of prayer was so powerful that I had to come tell you thank you in person. Prayer is powerful. Believe it, live it. It changed my life for the better."

Describing these moments is impossible because it was like I wasn't in control. I was there, my mouth was moving, it was my voice that they heard, but it wasn't coming from me. The words that formed in my mind and tumbled out of my mouth were from

Someone else's thoughts. I don't know how else to explain what happened that day.

The faces before me were transfixed. There wasn't a sound to be heard in that room; even the kids were quiet. Quiet tears washed down some cheeks and other people nodded encouragement.

When I finished speaking and sat down, I wasn't tired. I wasn't shaking. My left arm didn't hurt. Brother Dale asked me to stand by the doors and I had energy to shake hands and smile and meet these wonderful people. Young and old, I enjoyed meeting each of them and was blessed, not exhausted by it. Something had changed.

Looking back, I realize that I had found my purpose.

CHAPTER NINE

Turning Around

THERE IS NOT A DAY THAT I DON'T THINK, Why not *me?* Why, when other people had families and I was still a single man, why was it that I was selected to live; that I won the life lottery and they didn't?

So many others who died that day had a lot of people counting on them. It just didn't add up for me. It still doesn't add up, but I've learned that it is what it is. There's no changing what happened, there's no changing my location back that day. I can't say, "I'll swap with you." But if I could have ever switched with one of those people who had a family counting on them, I would have.

Soon my questions and prayers began to have answers. Although I didn't have a family of my own, I began to see my impact in the world.

One of the 4-H programs I run with my local group deals with public speaking. As a speaker myself, it's my favorite programs with the kids. My favorite memory about the many kids I've mentored through the years is the story of one girl who reminded me how important a few words spoken out loud can truly be.

The title of this young girl's 4-H project was "Organic Eggs." If you were to hear that title, there's no way you would think that it would be a life-affirming and engrossing speech! Of course, it seems like a farm thing, related to 4-H, right? But in this case, it wasn't about farming or the club. It was about her father, who was dying of cancer. She had read that organic eggs have proteins in them that would help fight the cancerous tumors in her father. So that's why she wanted organic eggs to be the subject of her speech. She wanted to help her dad.

I found out her touching story, and I was thinking, we're going to deliver the best speech of her life. We both dove into researching organic eggs. I couldn't have cared a lick about them before, but now, I can tell you, I knew just about everything you would ever want to know about an organic egg. Why? Because this girl had something to believe in greater than herself, and I had the opportunity to help her believe. That was my mission.

She and I could both tell you about the nutrients in every egg, and what the mother hens were allowed to eat and why. I can still tell you everything about an organic egg, because she put that spark into me. It was her passion, and it quickly became mine, as her mentor on the speech.

Long story short, she won the local competition. After that, I told her that we're only halfway there. We had a county competition coming up. So we prepared and we practiced, and her dad was in the other room dying as we were rehearsed. She was devoted to this, and I was sure that she would give the speech of her life.

We were going to the county competition, and she would be competing against the other top kids in 4-H. Even though she was only ten years old, she would be delivering this speech about eggs and her father in front of a huge audience. She won the entire competition. She beat out some of the best young speakers I've ever heard in competition. And what did she do?

The first thing the young girl did after she won the county competition was call her father. She said, "Dad, I won." I heard on the other end of the line as her father said, "I'm so proud of you."

At that moment, I saw that this meant everything to this girl and her father. You could see it. I mean, she felt like she had made a difference.

I stood there next to this ten-year-old girl, and I realized at that moment, "Oh my God, this is one of the greatest things in the world. This is why I was saved on 9/11." I knew that she had made her father truly happy, and she had done everything in her power to honor and heal her father.

Her father passed away only weeks later. The girl was asked to deliver the eulogy at her father's memorial service.

Her father had been a firefighter, and thousands of people came to pay their respects. This little girl stood in front of them and honored her father, who had finally succumbed to cancer after a long fight.

The little girl's mother looked up at me as I walked by, and her eyes said it all. Like Erin Anderson, who had driven Bobby and me away from the burning Pentagon, as if she had been the answer to my prayers, I was blessed to work with this precocious girl. She would then be able to eulogize her father, and honor his memory.

The feeling that you get when you've made somebody's life a little better is amazing. That is something I learned at a young age, and I continue learning it today.

Before 9/11, my mission in life would have been to live as happily as I possibly could, making a difference with what I could do.

But my mission on September 12th was to answer the question, "Why did I live?" I had to figure out why I was spared. Why did I live while others did not? Why does my life not have any meaning anymore? Why is this pain causing me to want to end everything?

Everything that I thought was what it was wasn't any more. Everything that I put value in didn't have it any more.

Now, the mission for the rest of my life is to help people go through this kind of process without having to go through what I did; to help them better understand their mission and purpose in life. I had to find my purpose again, and like a puzzle of what I thought my mission was beforehand, during 9/11 my puzzle pieces of life just went up in the air. They wouldn't fit any more when they came back down. Nothing made sense, but over the years, little by little, I put the pieces back again.

I found that the more I gave back, the more it felt like I was able to find a little bit of happiness. It was like the inside of me, my emotional state, was a wreck. I was one hell of a mess, and I didn't know which way was up or down. Telling people my story didn't help. Then I went to therapy, and that was when I realized that I had to start changing the way that I looked at things in life. It helped a lot to understand post-traumatic stress disorder and its effects.

Everything changed on 9/11, but I am rebuilding with forethought, care and appreciation. Now I can say that my life is better than it has ever been, or could ever have been if I hadn't experienced 9/11.

I want to bring up the point that I end with at most of my speeches. We all have our 9/11 moments in life. They are of varying degrees, of course, and I hope that others won't have to experience the horror that we experienced in the Pentagon that day. But, we all have that moment in our lives when we are forced to stop and say, "Oh my God, what does my life mean at this moment in time?"

For me, 9/11 had been such a normal September day. How could I ever have guessed that a plane would hit the building where I worked? That my life would change forever from that moment forwards?

I never knew how great my life could be after a plane hit me. I was so stuck in the doldrums of depression and post-traumatic stress after the attack that I didn't think my life could ever return to normal, let alone be *better* than it was before.

I can now say with certainty that we don't find out how great things can be until we almost lose it all. There I was on death's doorstep, fighting for my life. I had never realized how precious time is, how ultimately valuable life is, and how important people around me are. I had never really appreciated everyone in my life, like I do today.

One nanosecond of impact changed my life forever.

184 people died right next to me, and I think about them all every day and every night.

Those of us who survived were reborn into a new life filled with appreciation.

Without Erin Anderson coming to our rescue; without having my camp available; without having the church available—it would have been impossible.

I would never take back that day, as horrible as it was. I would never want to go back to the life I used to live, because I was missing out on so much of my life and I didn't even know it.

9/11 forced me to look at my life as I had never had the ability to do before. I could never have conceptualized hitting a stop button in my life and saying out loud to myself, "Am I doing everything that I really should be doing with my life? Am I appreciating everything that I have? Is there something missing in my life?" How about you?

I had been living the life in Washington in my beautiful apartment overlooking the city. I had everything paid for; it was a sweet deal. I was the person that you could describe to other people as being successful, and I did everything to make sure I looked the part. My company wanted to throw me right up the corporate ladder, not have me climb it. But I was living my life for everybody else.

In that way, 9/11 was a gift to me. Awful things happened on that day, but I can honestly never look back and say it was the worst day of my life. Sure, I still have pains in my sides, and I still have a few after-effects from the blast. But the real gift I received on that day was the gift of appreciation. I now have the ability to be thankful for everything that I have. And I never forget that.

Others have that same experience every day. If you want to appreciate life, go volunteer at an oncology ward. Go see people fighting for their lives. Do you think you're entitled to three square meals a day? Go volunteer at a soup kitchen and watch people appreciate every bite of food. That's what life is.

Some people now look at me and say, "That guy is nuts. Look how happy he is."

You know what, you're darn right I am. And there's nothing wrong with that. Yes, I have bad things happen in my life. But it's how we decide how it's going to affect us; whether we're going to rise above it or fall beneath.

When the world was shaking around me, the one thing that stuck with me, especially during my recovery, was my faith.

I just kept asking God, "Why did You save me?"

I now realize that the reason I lived is so that I can let people know that they need to appreciate life; that they don't need to go through what I did in order to understand that concept.

There are still days when I cry myself to sleep. But, it's not as often as it used to be, and it's getting better through time.

Whenever I have a bad day, I just look at my left hand, start moving it, and I tell myself, *I'm alive.* That's all I need.

CONCLUSION

I DON'T JUST SAY THAT WE SHOULD ALL love each other. That's not specific enough. When people ask me what my "message" is when I speak at different places, I tell them, "Don't forget to tell the people whom you care about most how you feel about them. There's not always a tomorrow to do that. We need to take our moments when we have them. And when you do that, you live with no regrets.

I almost didn't have the opportunity to tell my family members that I loved them that one more time. What would you tell your family member if you knew that they would never come home again?

I challenge you, the reader, to live your life with a sense of purpose. If you need help defining that purpose, donate yourself to those that need you most, and that purpose will come alive. Don't wait for tomorrow to do everything that you know you can do today. Tomorrow may not be there.

Hang a sign above your bed with the word "appreciation" on it. Think about appreciation from the moment you wake up to the moment you put your head back on that pillow. Remember to appreciate what you have, and that you truly are not entitled to anything in life.

Just over two weeks after 9/11, my whole life changed again. I experienced the profound joy of holding my goddaughter Sydney in my hands only minutes after her birth.

I prayed a prayer of appreciation: "Thank you God for showing me how great life can be."

Now Sydney is a beautiful young girl, and the memory of 9/11 has grown into this story that I am writing for you, the reader.

Don't miss the moments that count most.

Think about newborn Sydney, or about your own experience seeing your child or grand-child, sister or brother just after birth, tiny and vulnerable. Embrace the gifts that life gives you each day, and appreciate them for everything that they are.

Work hard to never feel entitled to anything. Give thanks and have gratitude for everything that you receive. It will come back to you.

Sydney and I shared a minute or maybe two when she was only minutes old. Now we share much more, and I appreciate every minute of it. Just this morning, she sent me her first text message from her mom's phone, and I remem-bered how many moments I have to share with her now and for a lifetime to come.

I found something to live for on 9/11. I thought, *I've got to be alive to meet my little god-child.* I knew she would be born any day now. Through all of the pain and the chaos of the wreckage after the blast, I thought about my sister and the child I was supposed to meet.

Let go of what you think life is supposed to be—all the premonitions, all the expectations. Let it all go and just be who you are, and not what anyone else thinks you are. Have faith in yourself, give your appreciation freely, and always ask for help.

❖

Thank you to all of the people who helped me along the way. From getting me out of a burning building to sitting with me and listening to my story, I would not be here today without you. I hope that your giving will come back to you in manifold ways. I hope that you see a reflection of the goodness you gave me in what I now do each day.

ABOUT THE AUTHOR

DAN HOLDRIDGE, A LIFELONG BOSTON RED SOX FAN, serves as CEO of his family business in Rhode Island. He graduated from the University of Connecticut, and earned a Master's Degree in Engineering Management from the University of New Haven. Dan served as a Trustee of the National 4-H Leadership Trust from April 2002 to 2004 and currently serves as Board Member and Vice Chairman of the New London County 4-H Foundation. To contact Dan for a speaking engagement, visit www.DanHoldridge.com or call (401) 596-8111.